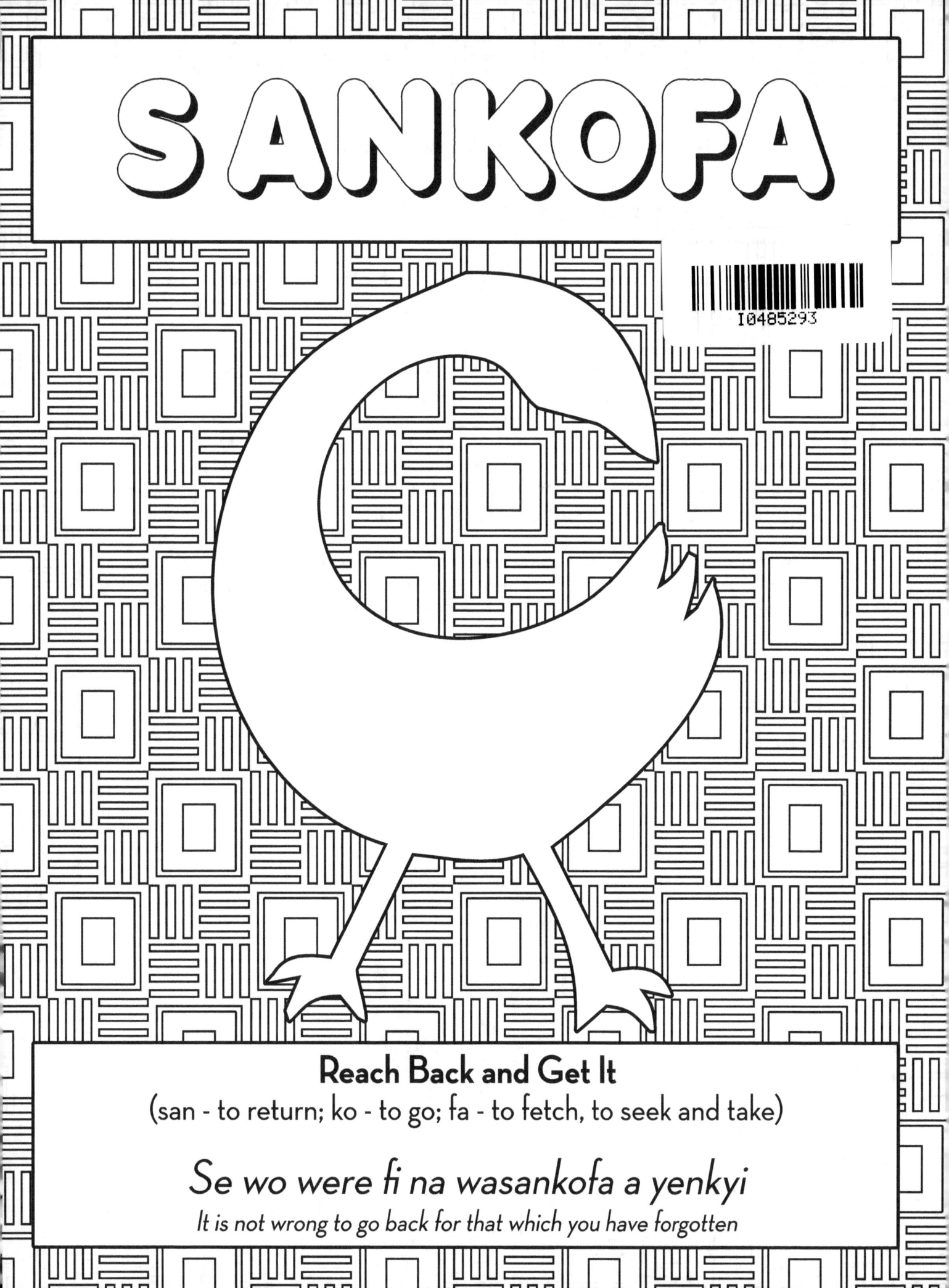

SANKOFA

I0485293

Reach Back and Get It
(san - to return; ko - to go; fa - to fetch, to seek and take)

Se wo were fi na wasankofa a yenkyi

It is not wrong to go back for that which you have forgotten

IN THE NAME OF GOD THE GRACIOUS AND THE MERCIFUL

ACKNOWLEDGEMENTS

My sincerest gratitude and thanks go God - the Glorified and Exalted, my mother, my Muslim community, and my global *AfRaKan* family.

Many people, unknowingly inspired this work and series.
They are educators, artist, activist, and advocates who teach, work for justice, and fulfill the needs their respective communities:
Mama Fiyah Like Ayanna, Epiphany Castro, Mama Mawusi Ashshakir, Ras Kofi da Farmah, Brother Manifest, Abdul Musawwir, Toiia Rukuni, and Nadir Owowale. If I could sum up in one word how you inspired this particular work, it would be, "Passion", but that would only be a glimpse. Hopefully, these two will suffice: THANK YOU.

A very special thanks goes to all my babies: The toddler, preschool, and school-age children who have blessed my life. I am honored to have worked for and with you. I was never your teacher as much as you were mine.

In gratitude daily
LADY KHADIJA

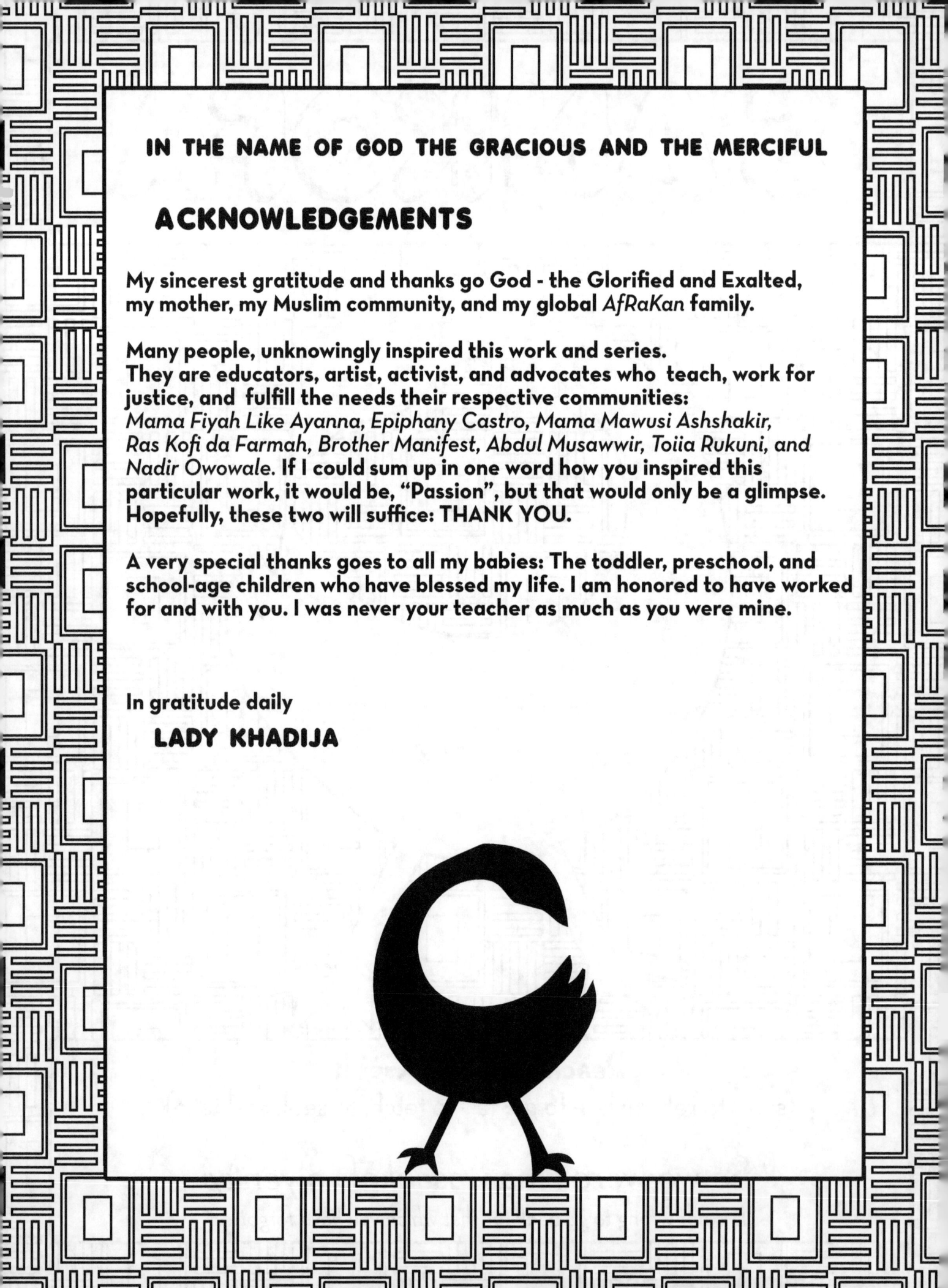

INTRODUCTION

This book is is intended for adults and children 12 and up. It is only an introduction to African culture for members of the diaspora and anyone interested in African prints, proverbs, and the diversity of our mother continent.

It is called Sankofa, but it barely scratches the surface of what we need to go back and retrieve. Our heritage and cultural legacy is very rich and intricate so, God willing, this work will be the first of a series of African centered and culturally inspired coloring books for adults and young people.

SOME BENEFITS OF COLORING

Coloring is a multi-sensory activity that stimulates the brain, develops motor skills, and enhances creativity. It have a very meditative effect, quieting the mind and relieving physical and emotional stress. It involves both logic and creativity, which activate both parts of the brain. Many psychologists have used coloring as relaxation techniques, citing that focusing on a single activity allows us to let go of worry, bring out our imagination , and go back to the happiest times of our childhood.

The benefits of coloring for children include, fine motor development, grasp learning, coordination, focusing on details, patience , planning, and preparation. Although these coloring pages may not be developmentally appropriate for all ages, they may be used as an introduction or supplement for other lessons and activities designed for young children. A companion book, Kente for Little Ones is the next to come in this *Sankofa Series.*

I hope this work serves you well.
Thank you.

LADY KHADIJA

THE PROVERBS

It is not wrong to go back for that which you have forgotten.
~From the Akan

Proverbs are the daughters of experience.
~From Sierra Leone/ Rwanda-Burundi

Before Shooting, one must aim.
~From Nigeria

He who learns, teaches.
~From Ethiopia

Unless you call out, who will open the door?
~From Ethiopia

Help me during the floods, I will help you during the drought.
~From Tanzania

Fine words do not produce food.
~From Nigeria

Talking with one another is loving one another.
~From Kenya

If relatives help each other, what evil can hurt them?
~From Ethiopia

If you mouth turns into a knife, it will cut off your lips.
~From Zimbabwe

He who talks incessantly, talks nonsense.
~From Ivory Coast

He who hunts two rats, catches none.
~From Buganda

If you watch your pot, your food will never burn.
~From Mauritania

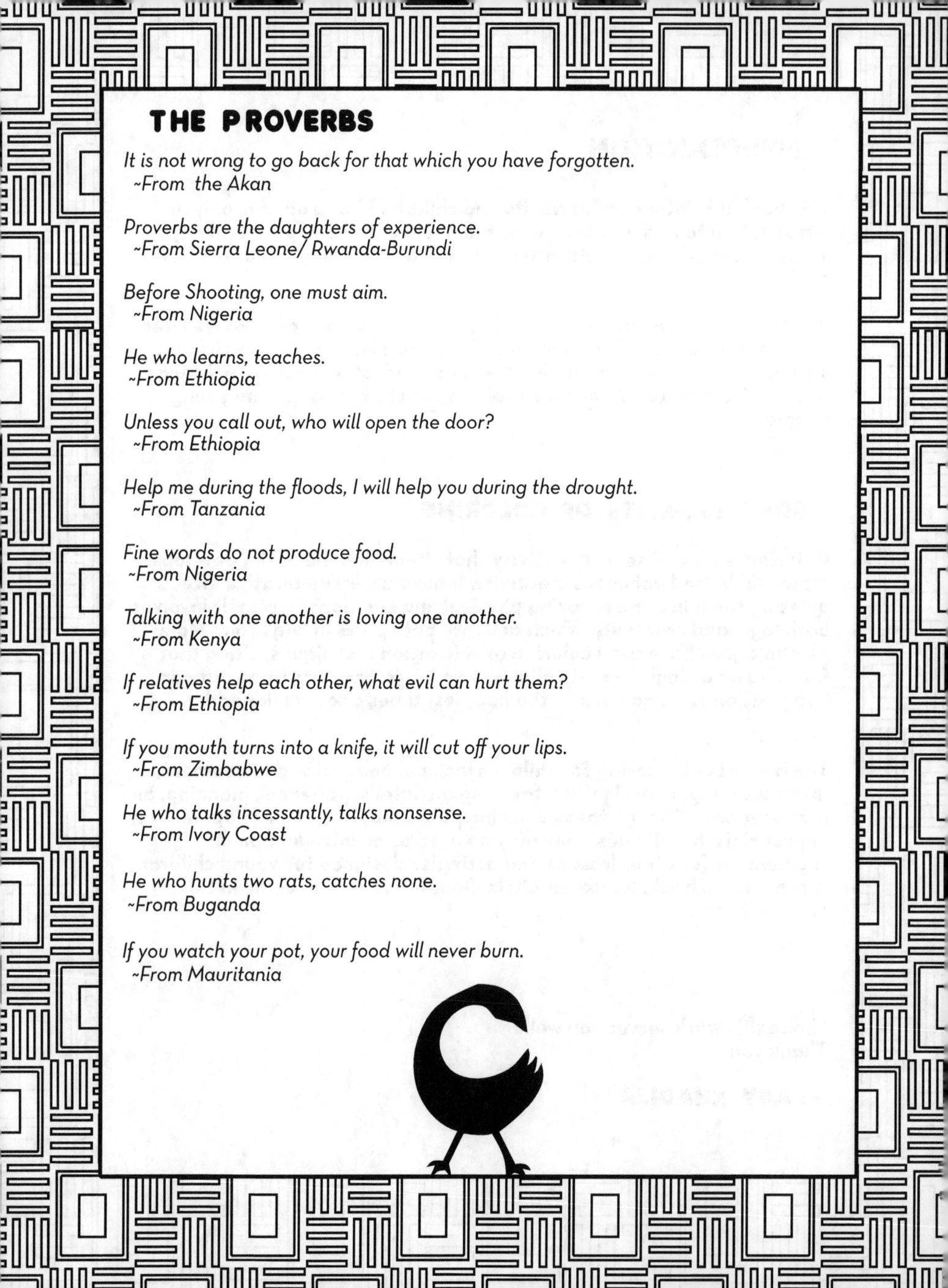

THE PROVERBS

One falsehood spoils a thousand truths.
~From the Ashanti

The most beautiful fig may contain a worm.
~From the Zulu

Spilled water is better than a broken jar..
~From Senegal

A little shrub may grow into a tree.
~From Sudan

He who does not cultivate his field will die of hunger.
~From Guinea

Scratch a lie, catch a theif.
~From the American South

The elephant who kills a rat is not a hero
~From Cameroon

Hold up that which holds you up.
~From the Congo

A roaring lion kills no game.
~From Uganda

It is no shame, at all, to work for money.
~From the Ashanti

A little rain, each day, will fill the rivers to overflowing.
~From Liberia

When spider webs unite, they can tie up a lion.
~From Ethiopia

Love is like a baby, it needs to be treated tenderly.
~From Zaire

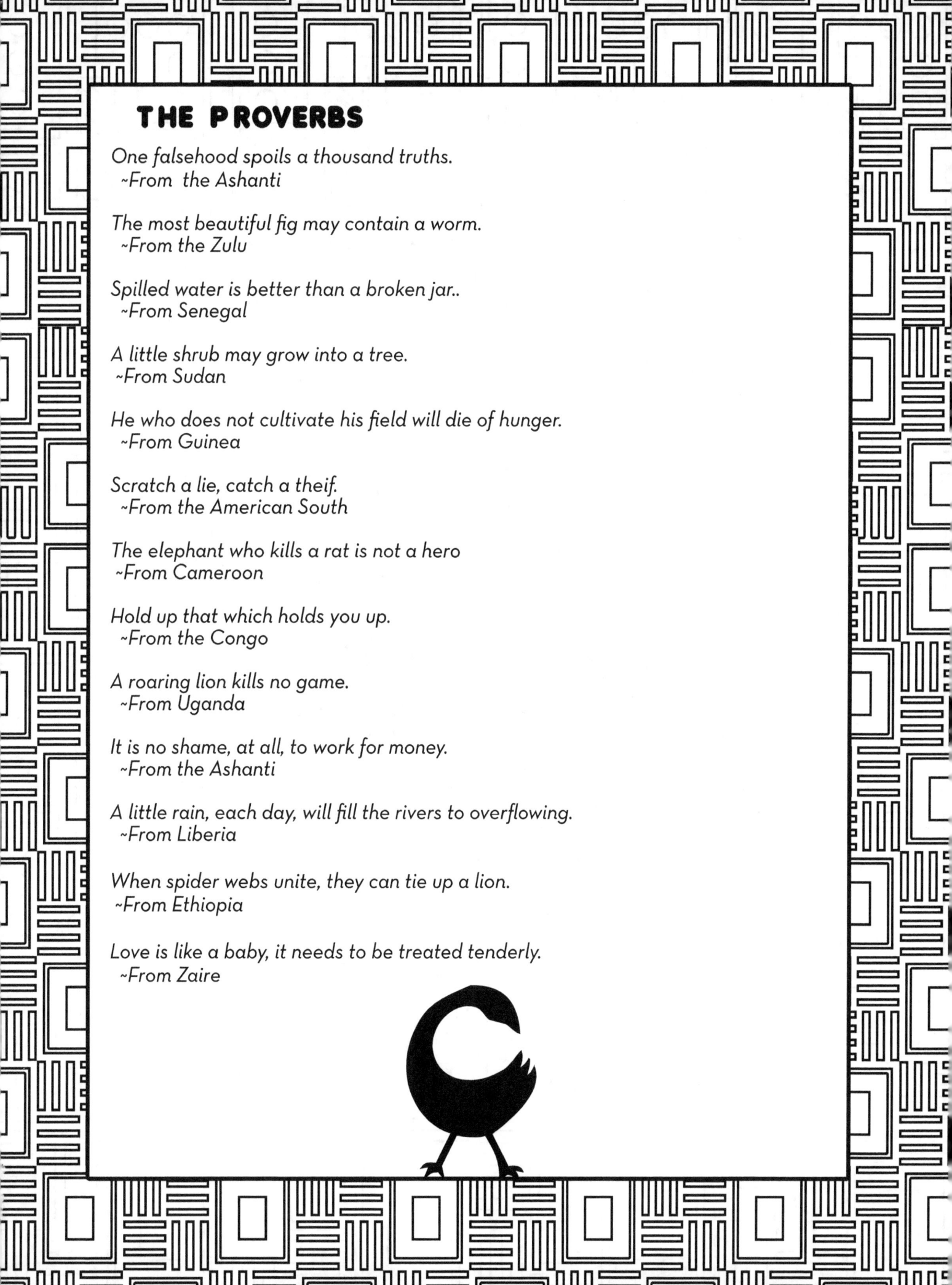

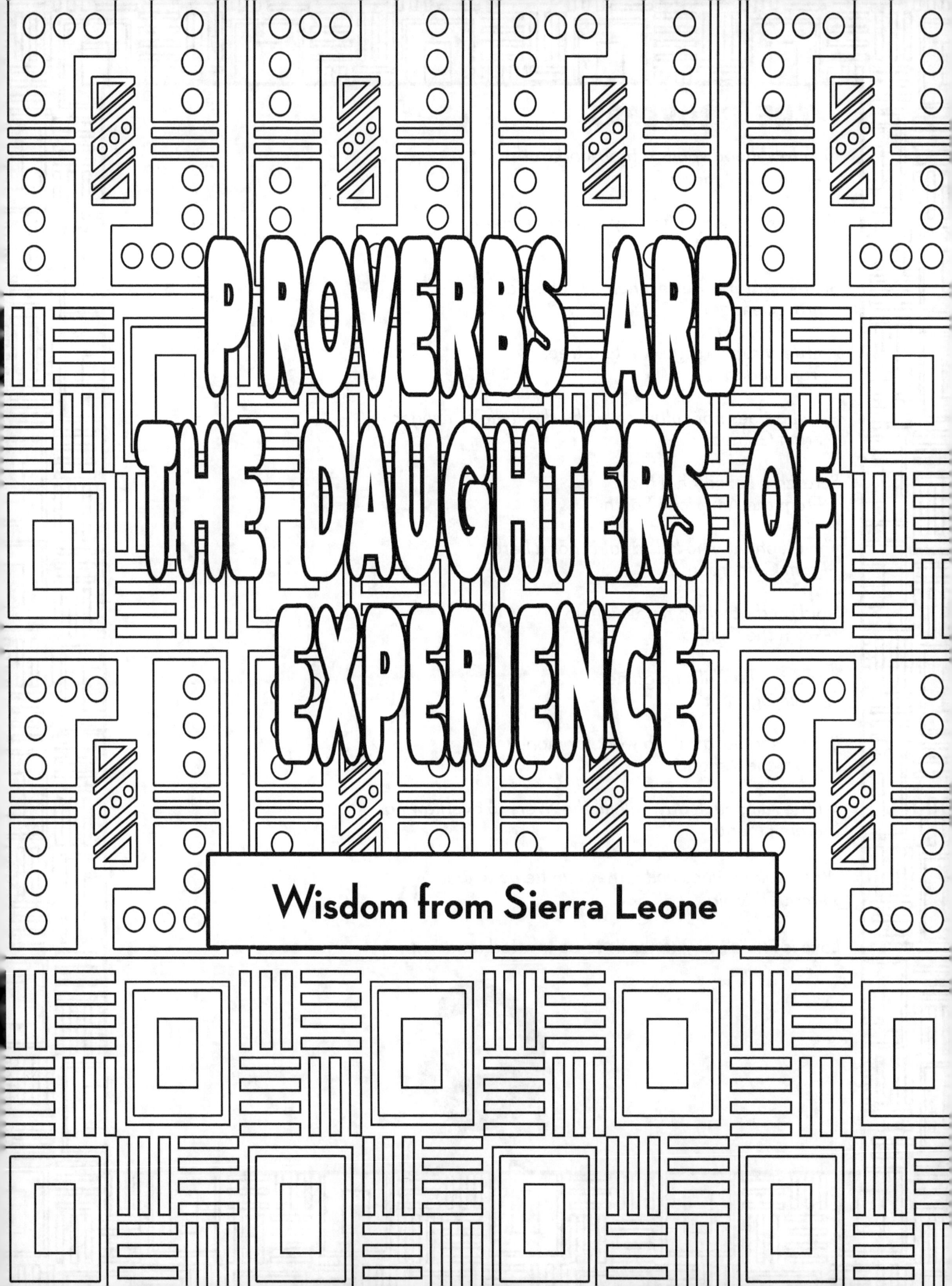

PROVERBS ARE THE DAUGHTERS OF EXPERIENCE

Wisdom from Sierra Leone

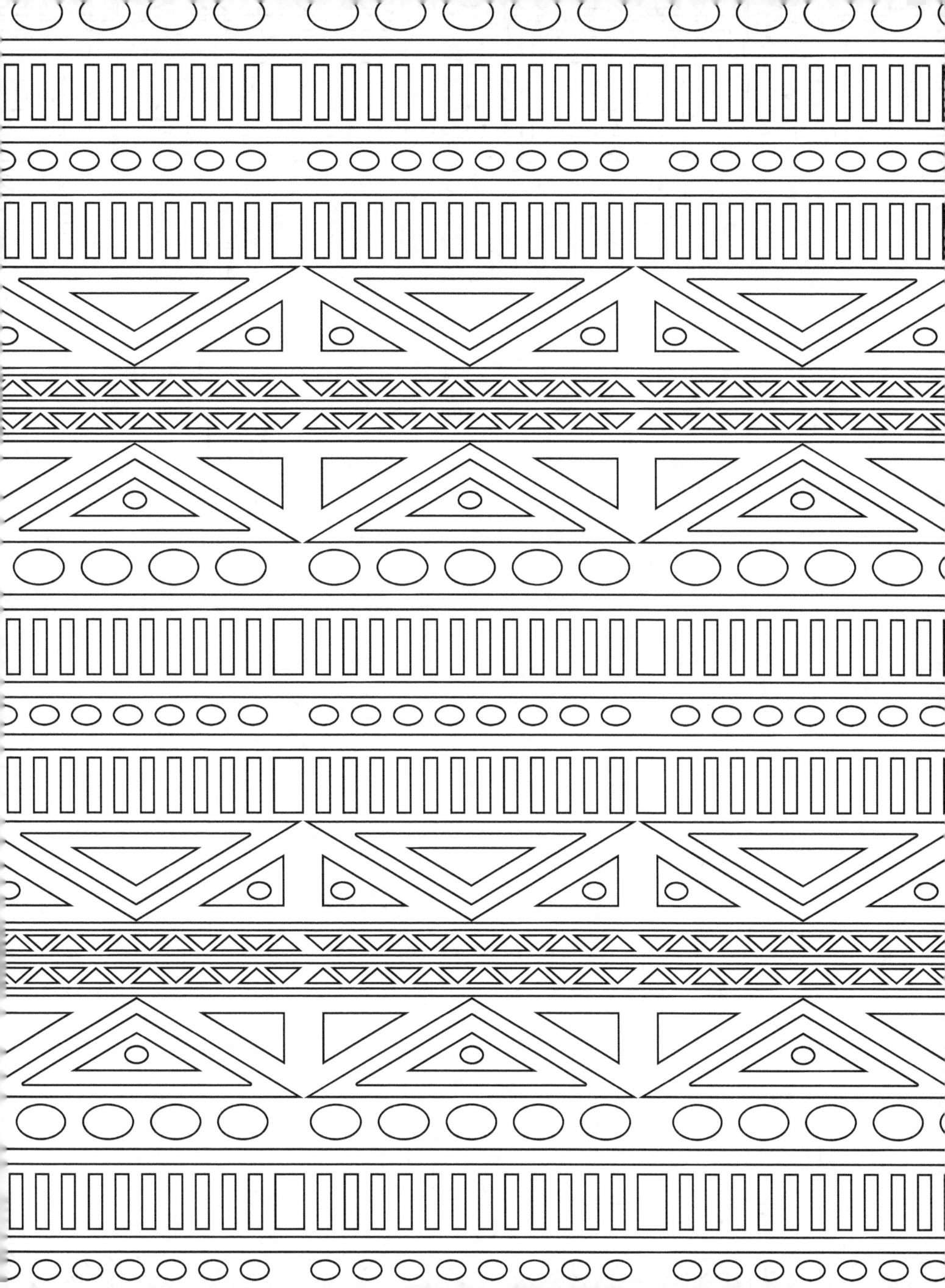

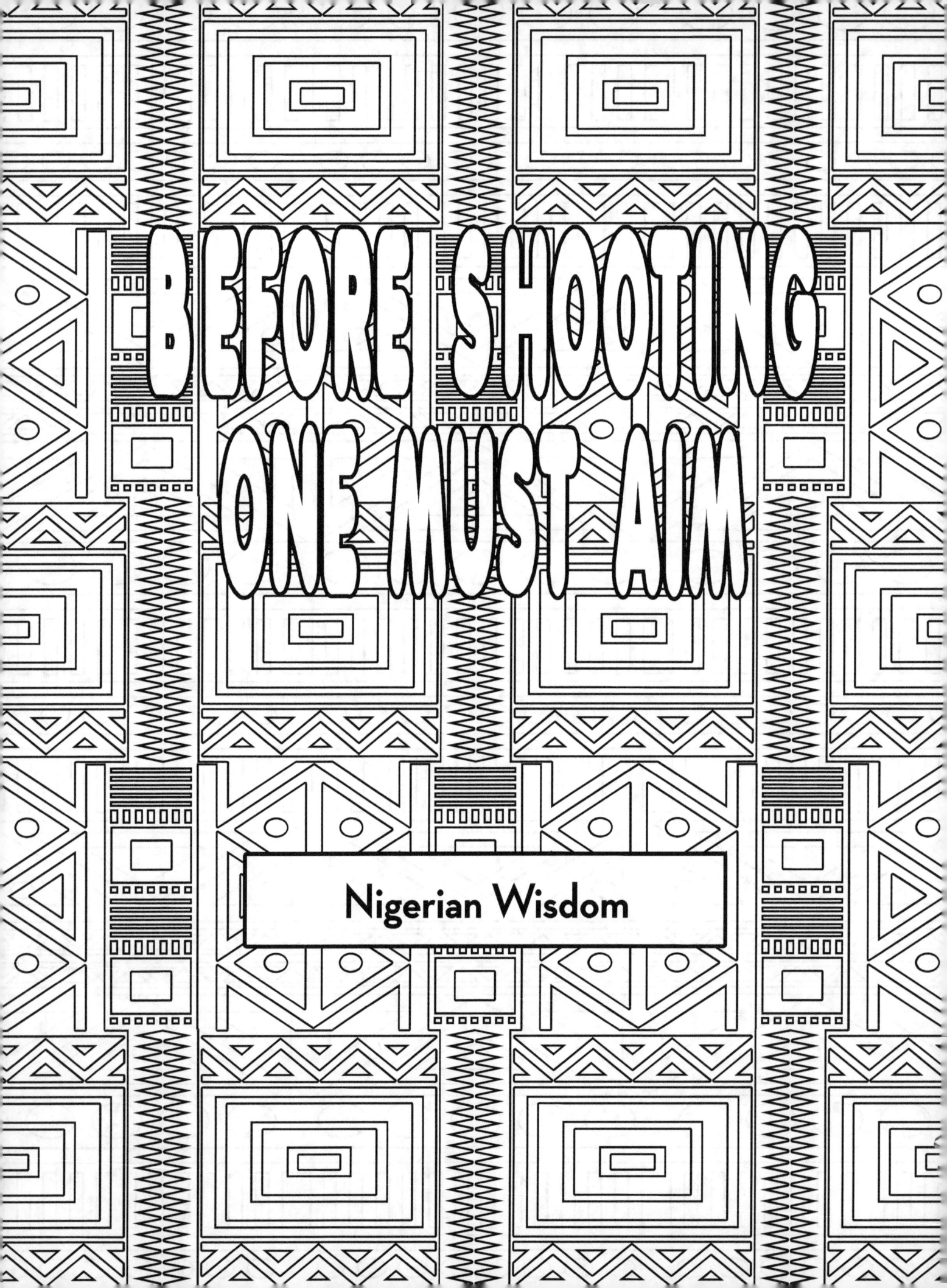

BEFORE SHOOTING ONE MUST AIM

Nigerian Wisdom

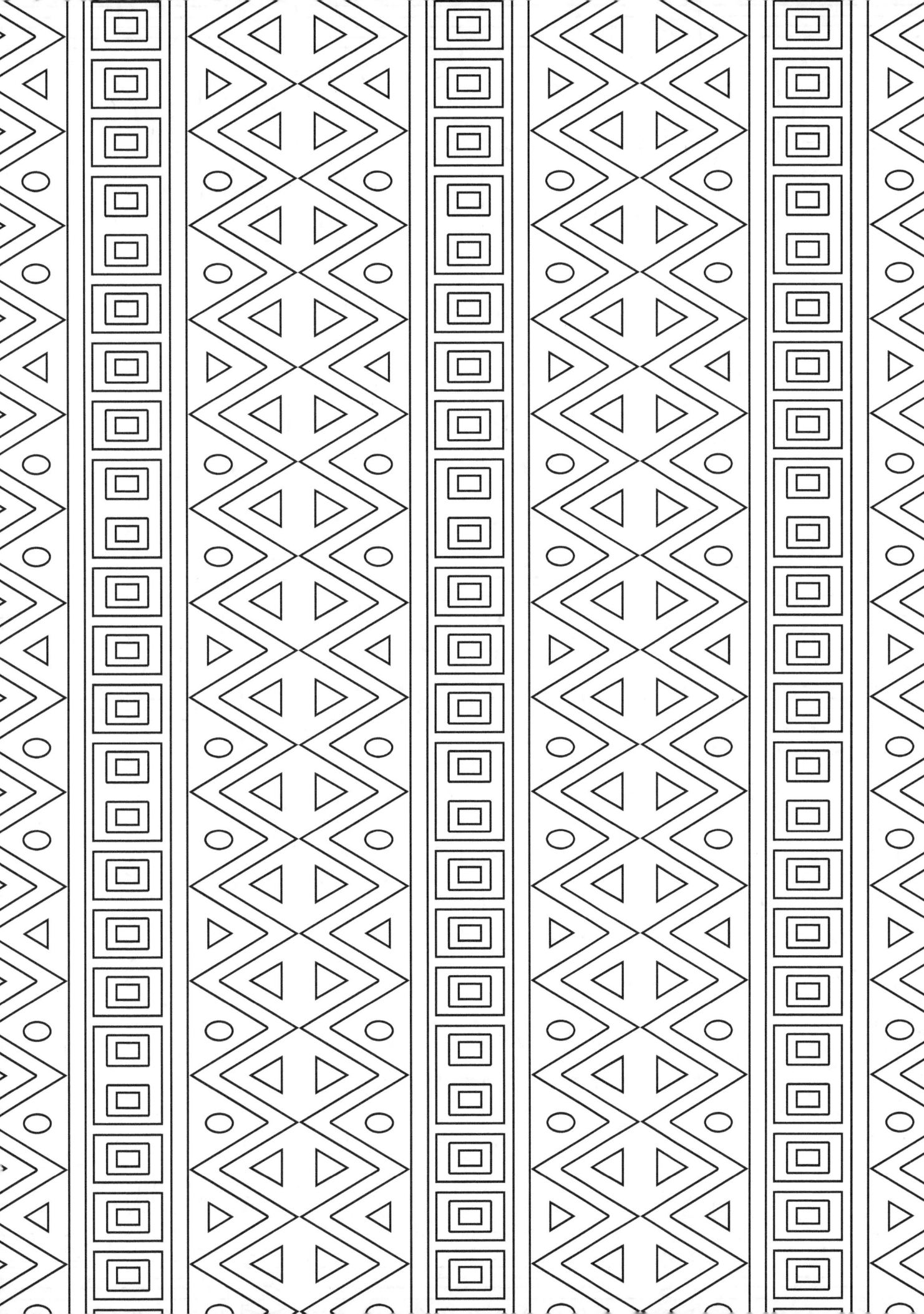

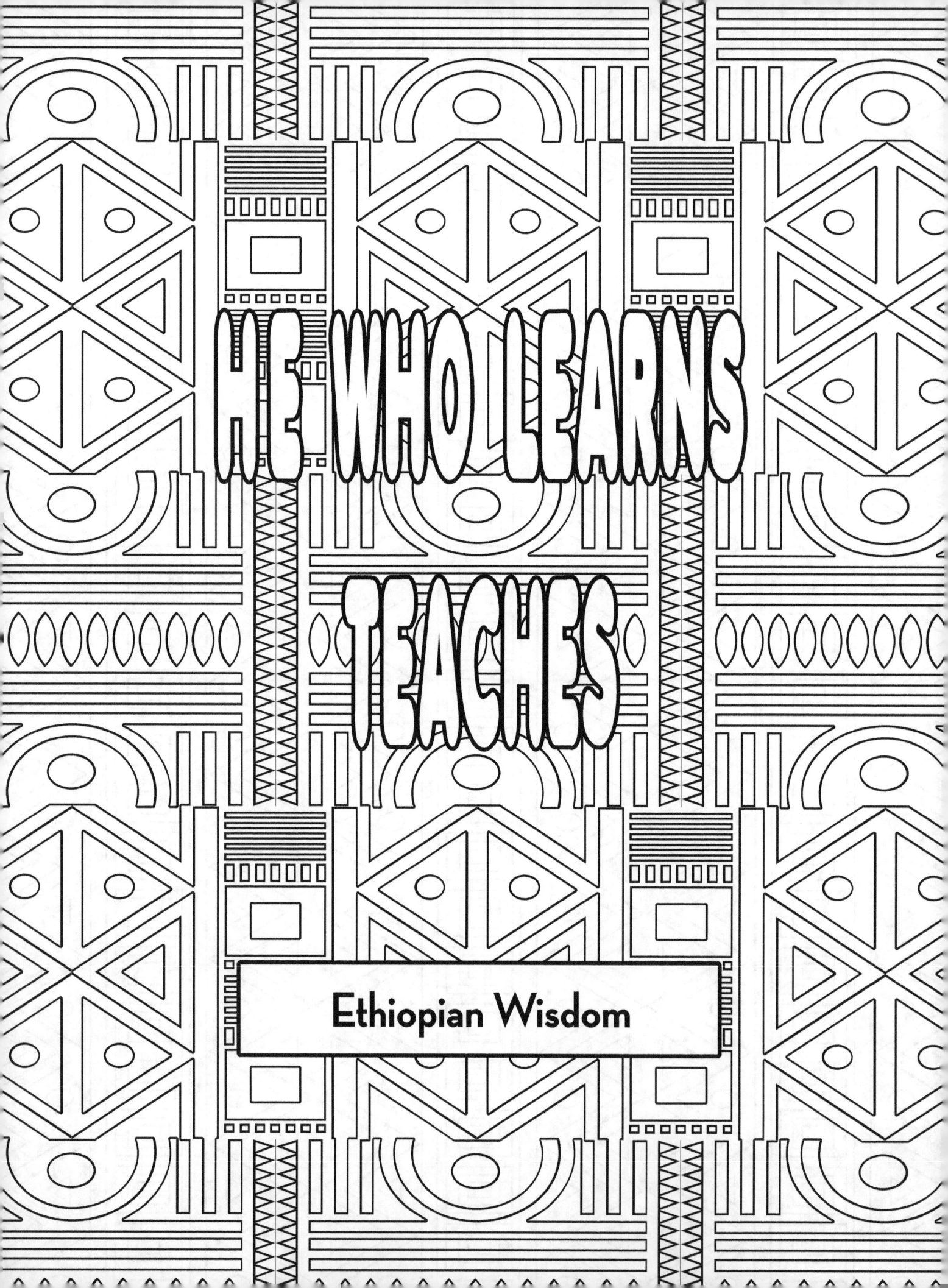

HE WHO LEARNS TEACHES

Ethiopian Wisdom

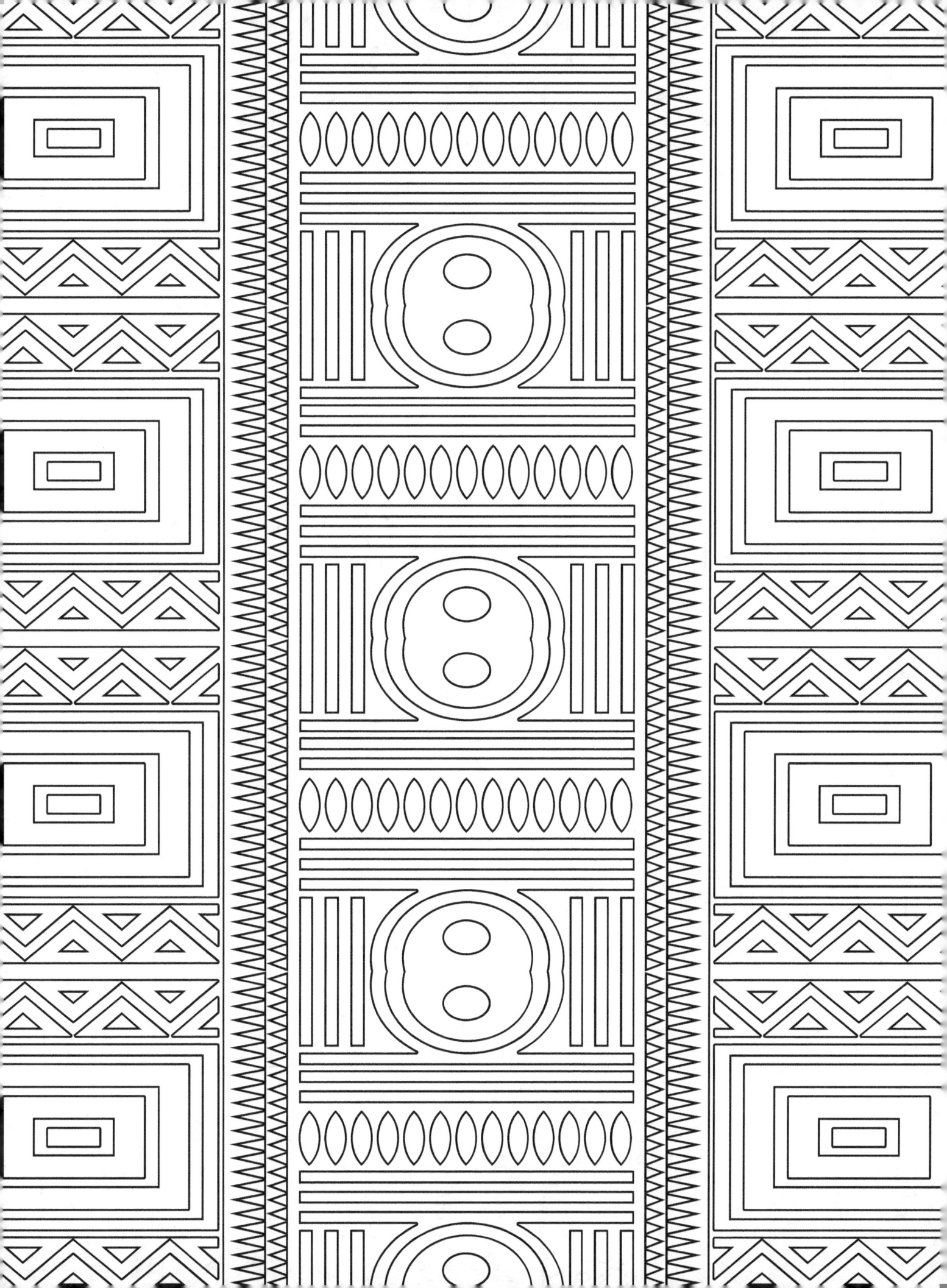

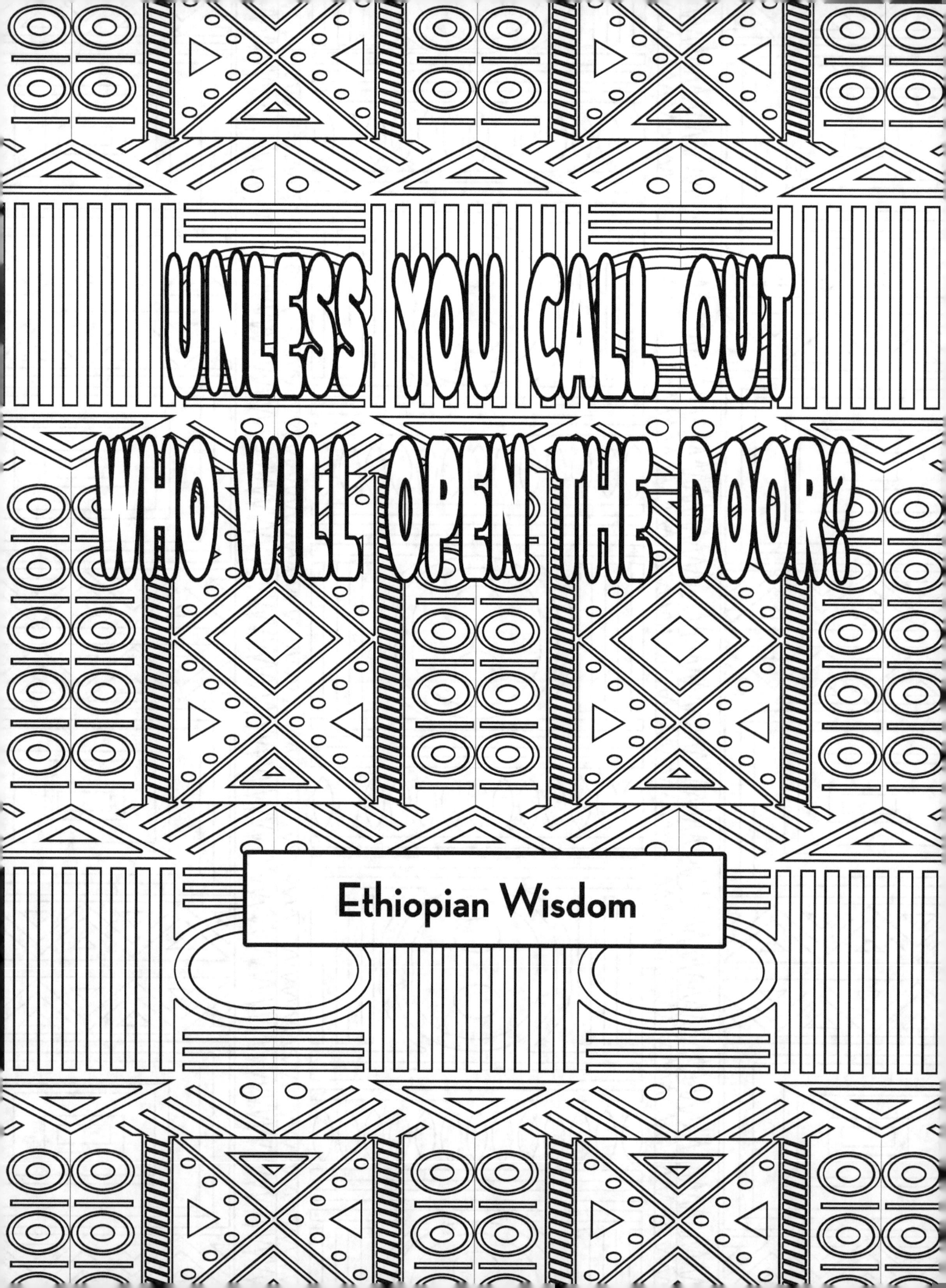

UNLESS YOU CALL OUT WHO WILL OPEN THE DOOR?

Ethiopian Wisdom

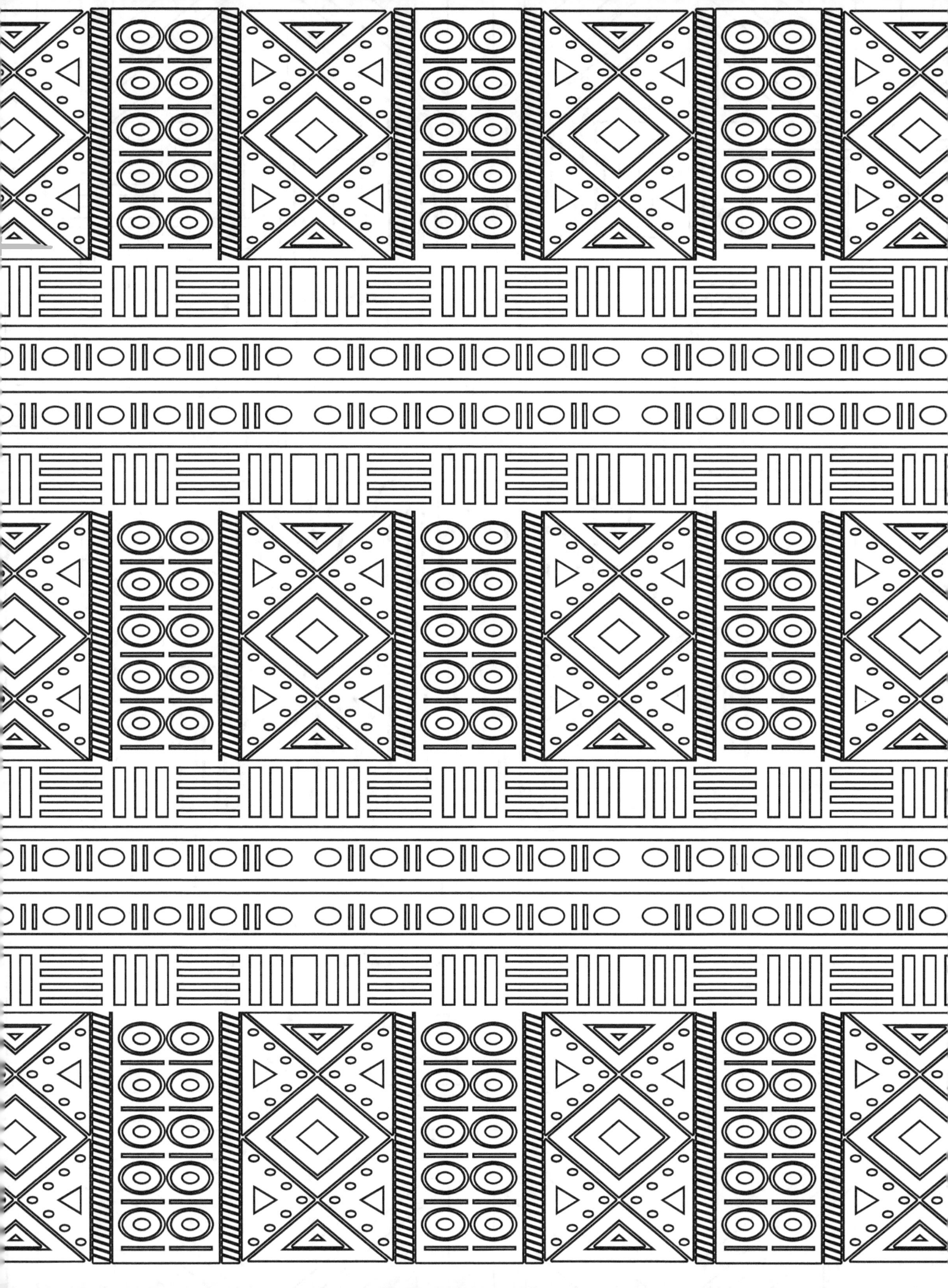

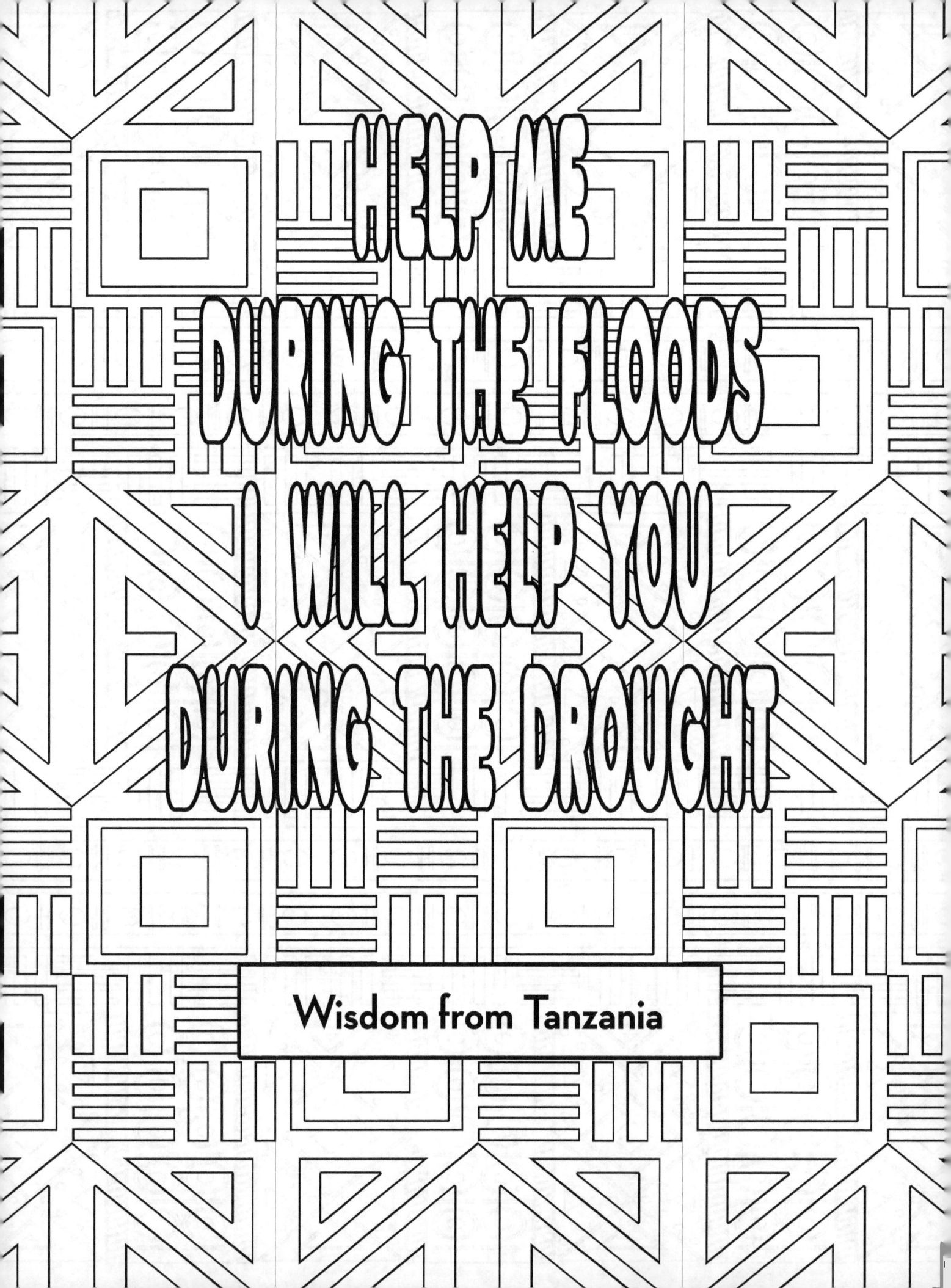

HELP ME DURING THE FLOODS I WILL HELP YOU DURING THE DROUGHT

Wisdom from Tanzania

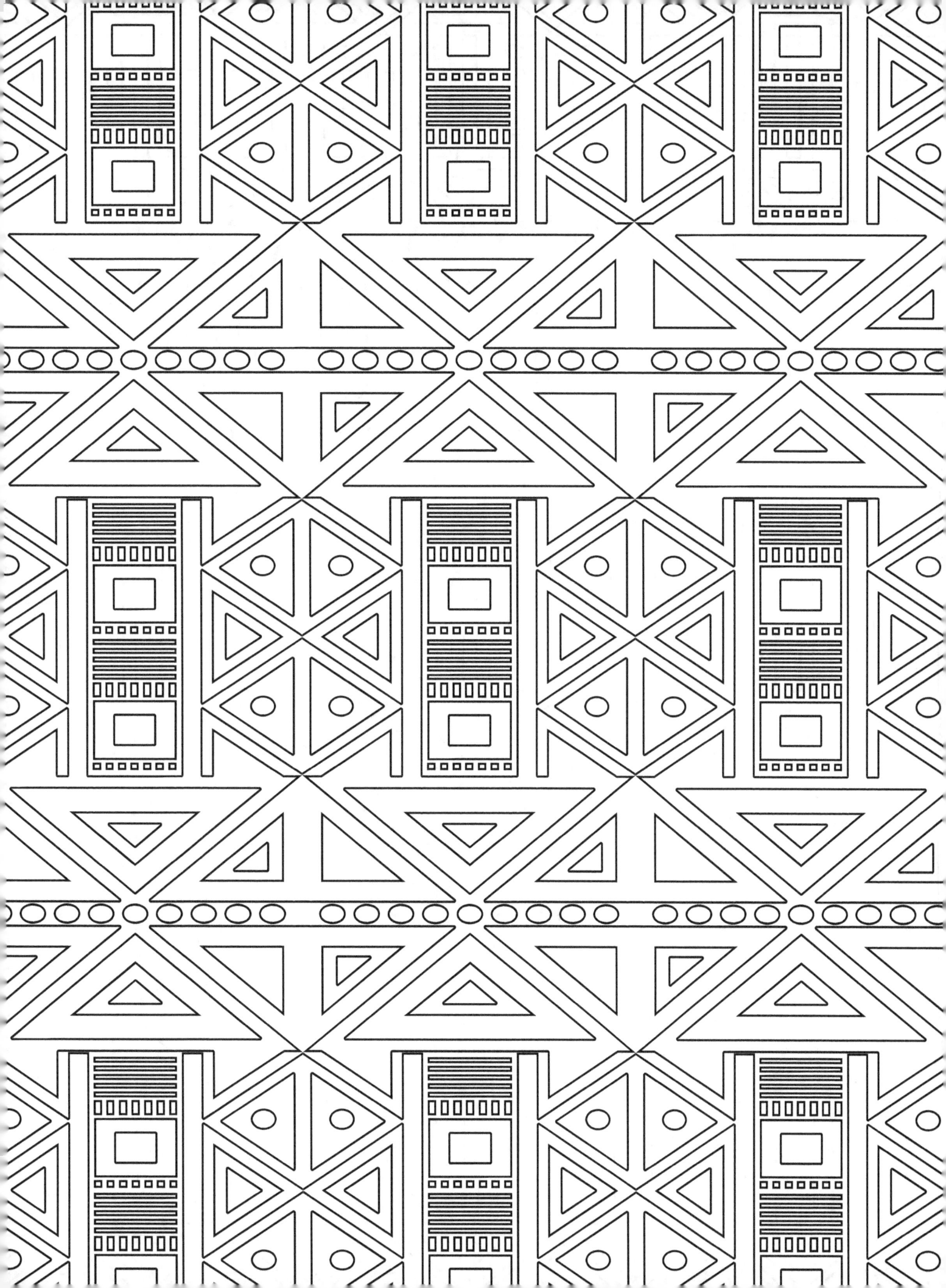

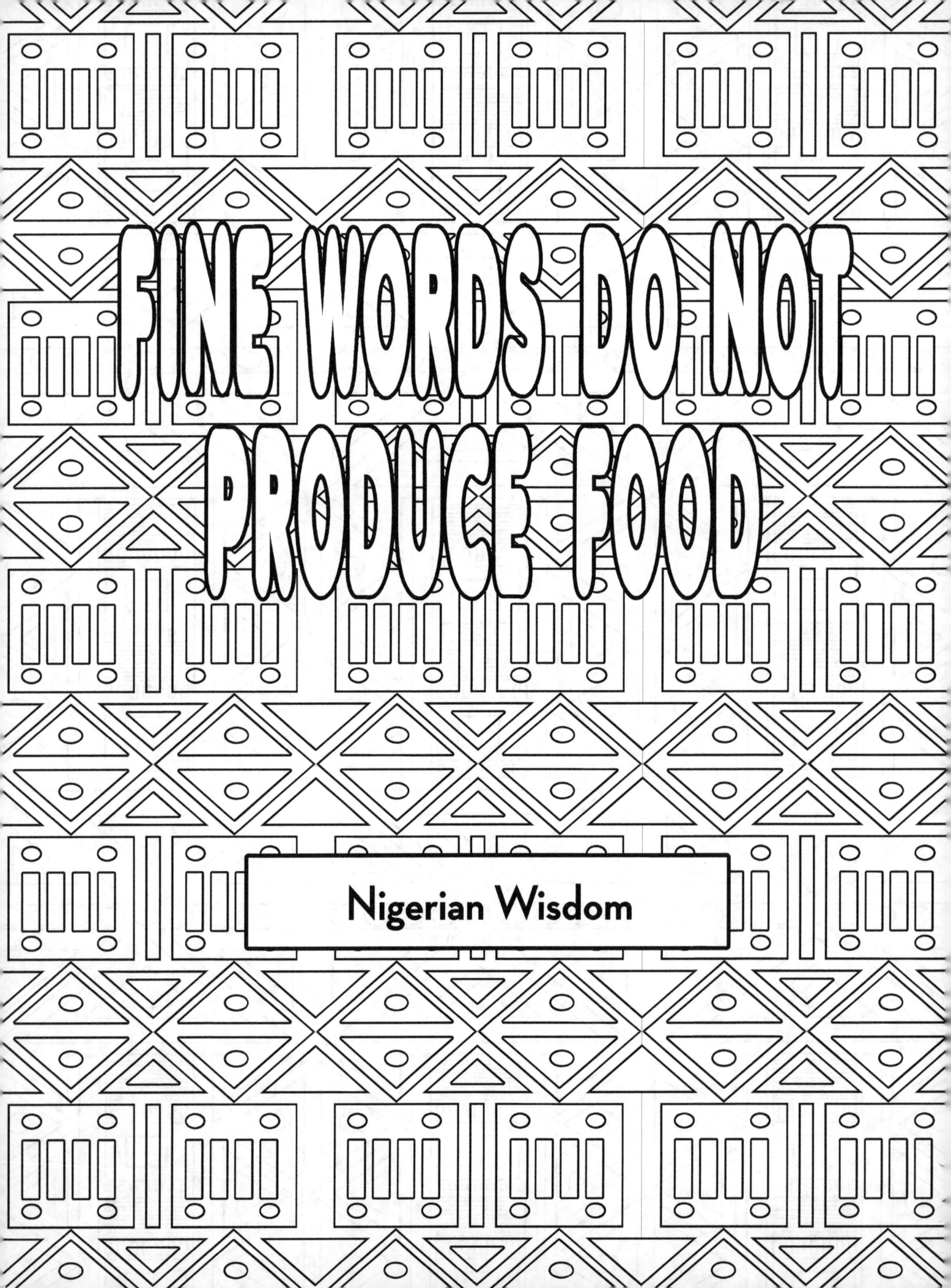

FINE WORDS DO NOT PRODUCE FOOD

Nigerian Wisdom

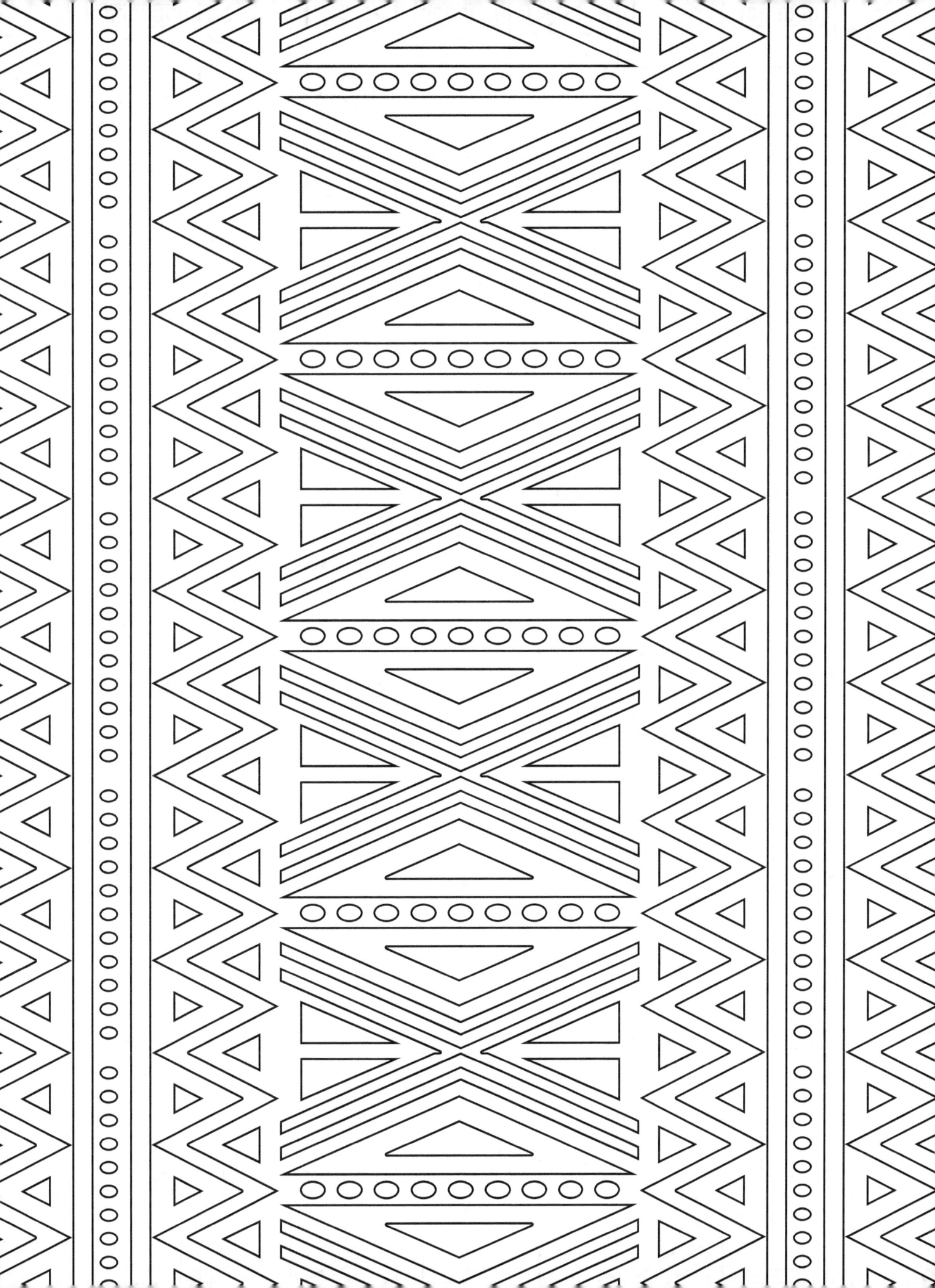

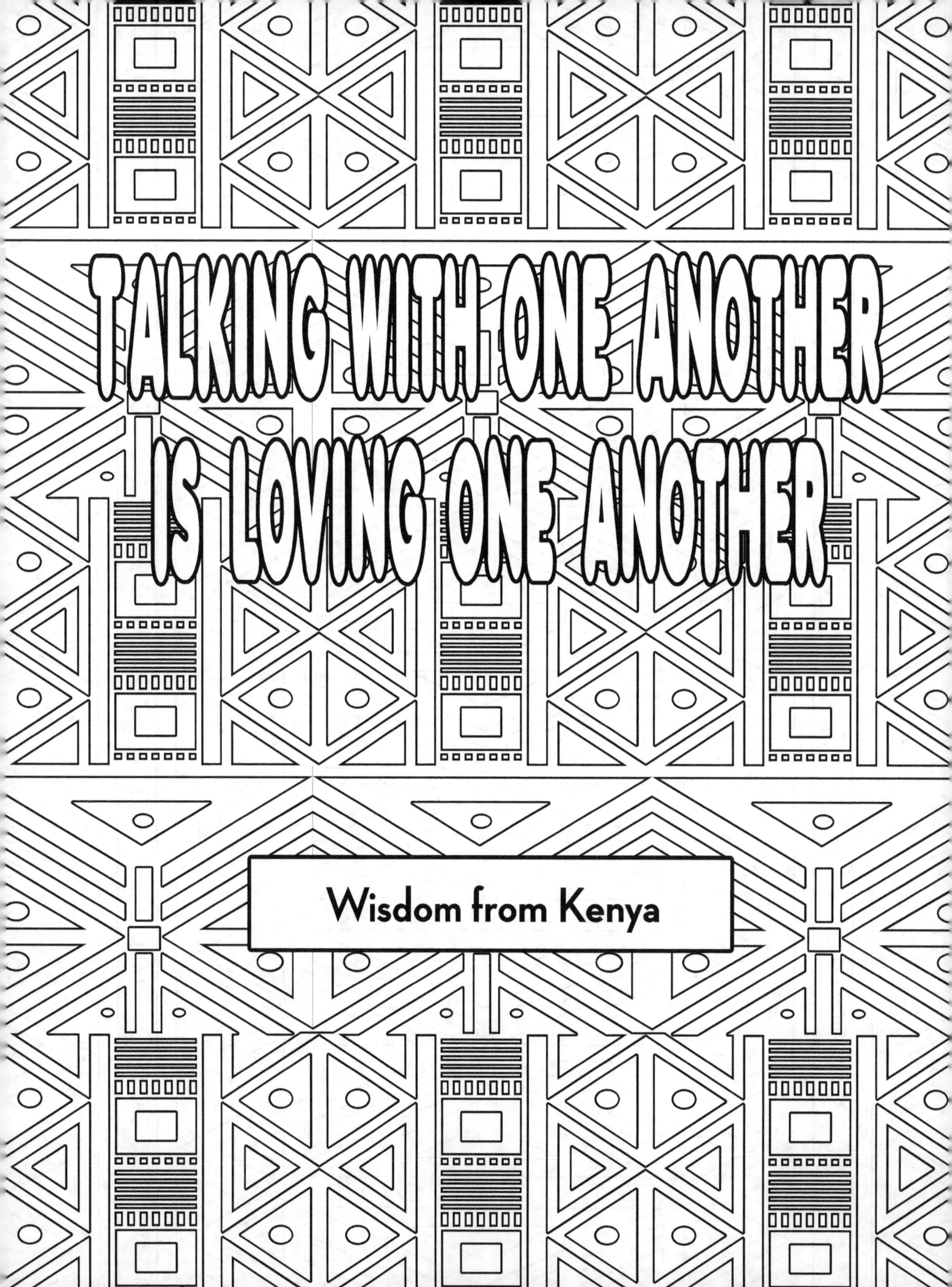

TALKING WITH ONE ANOTHER IS LOVING ONE ANOTHER

Wisdom from Kenya

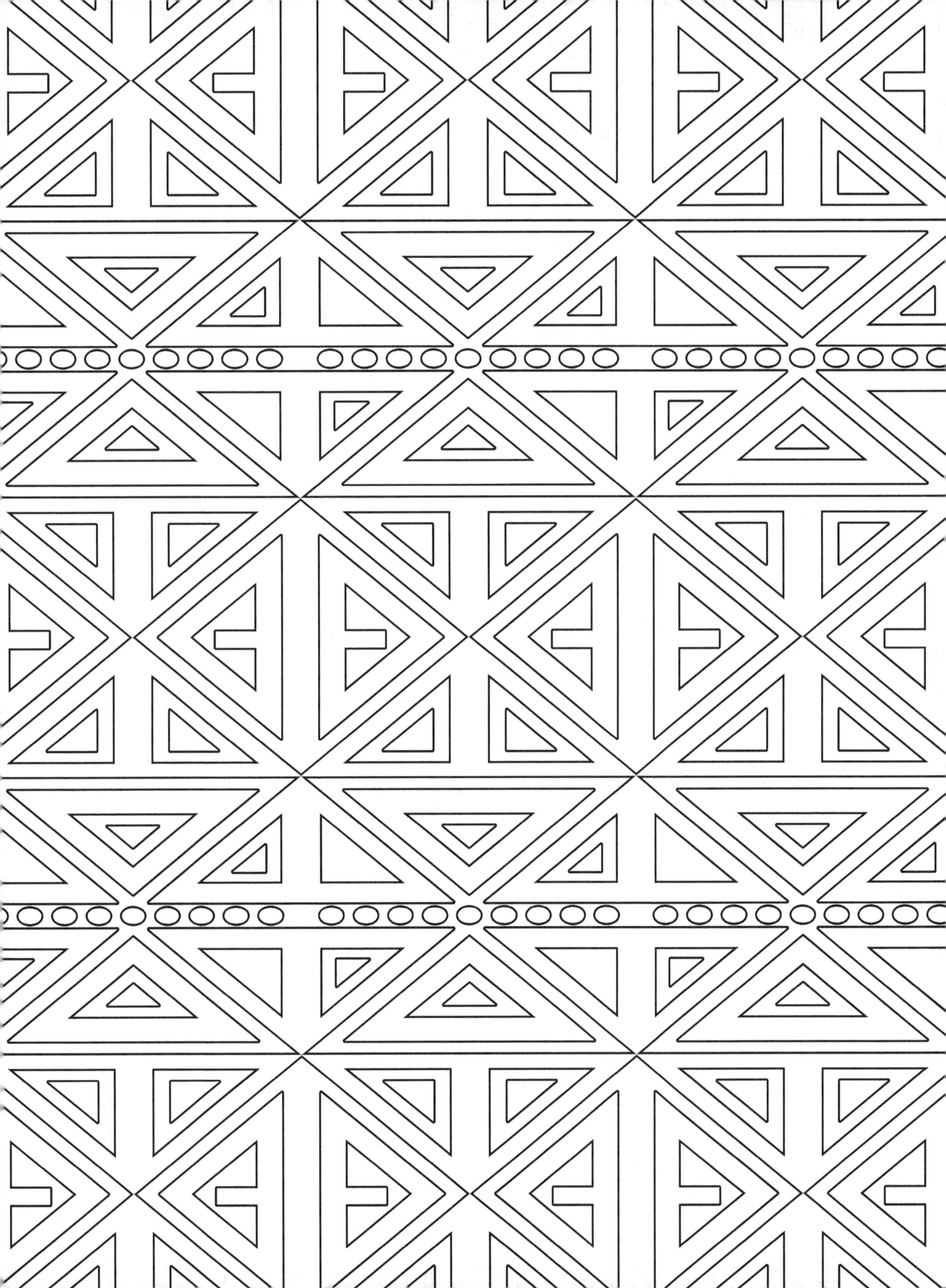

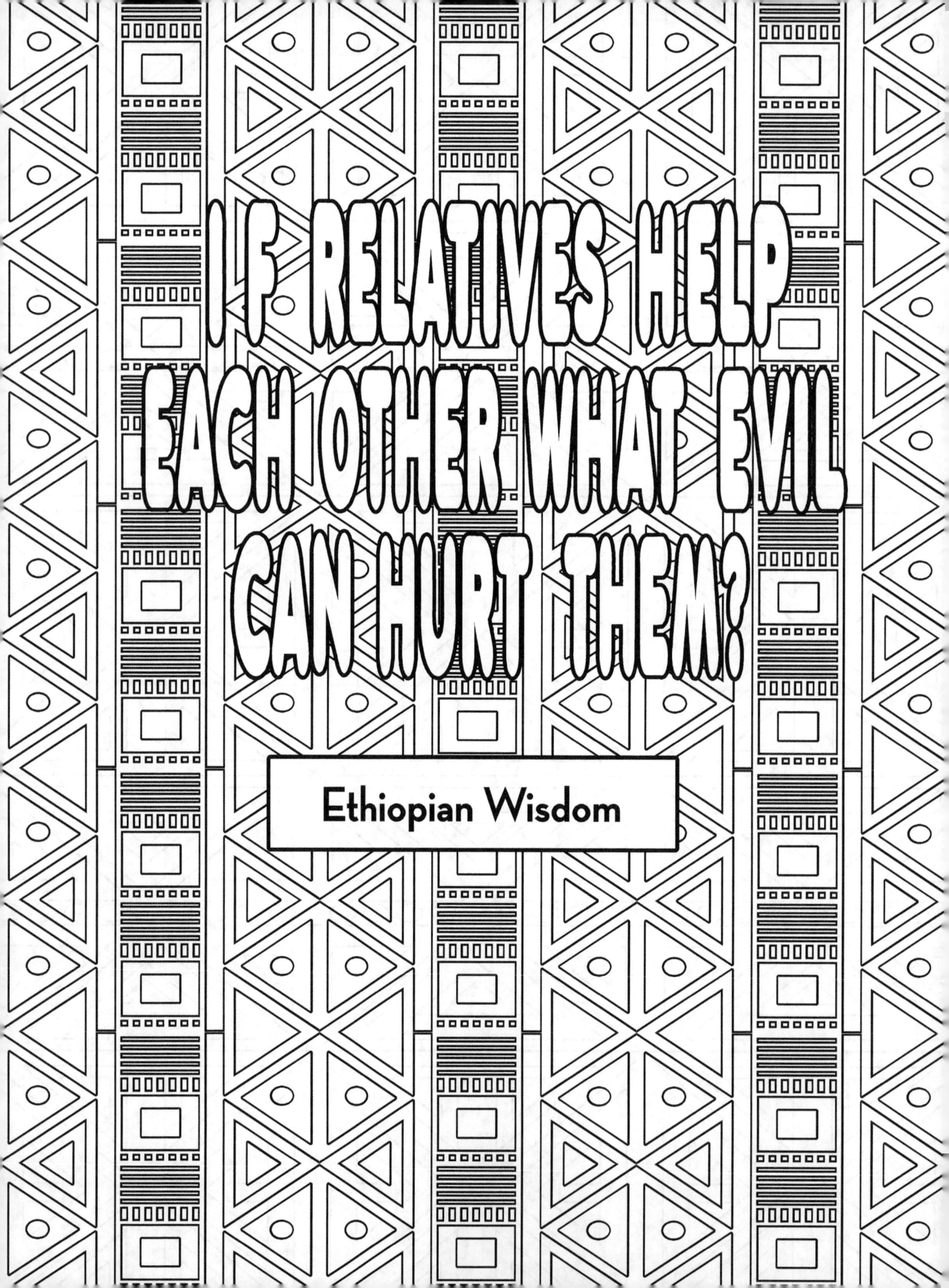

IF RELATIVES HELP EACH OTHER WHAT EVIL CAN HURT THEM?

Ethiopian Wisdom

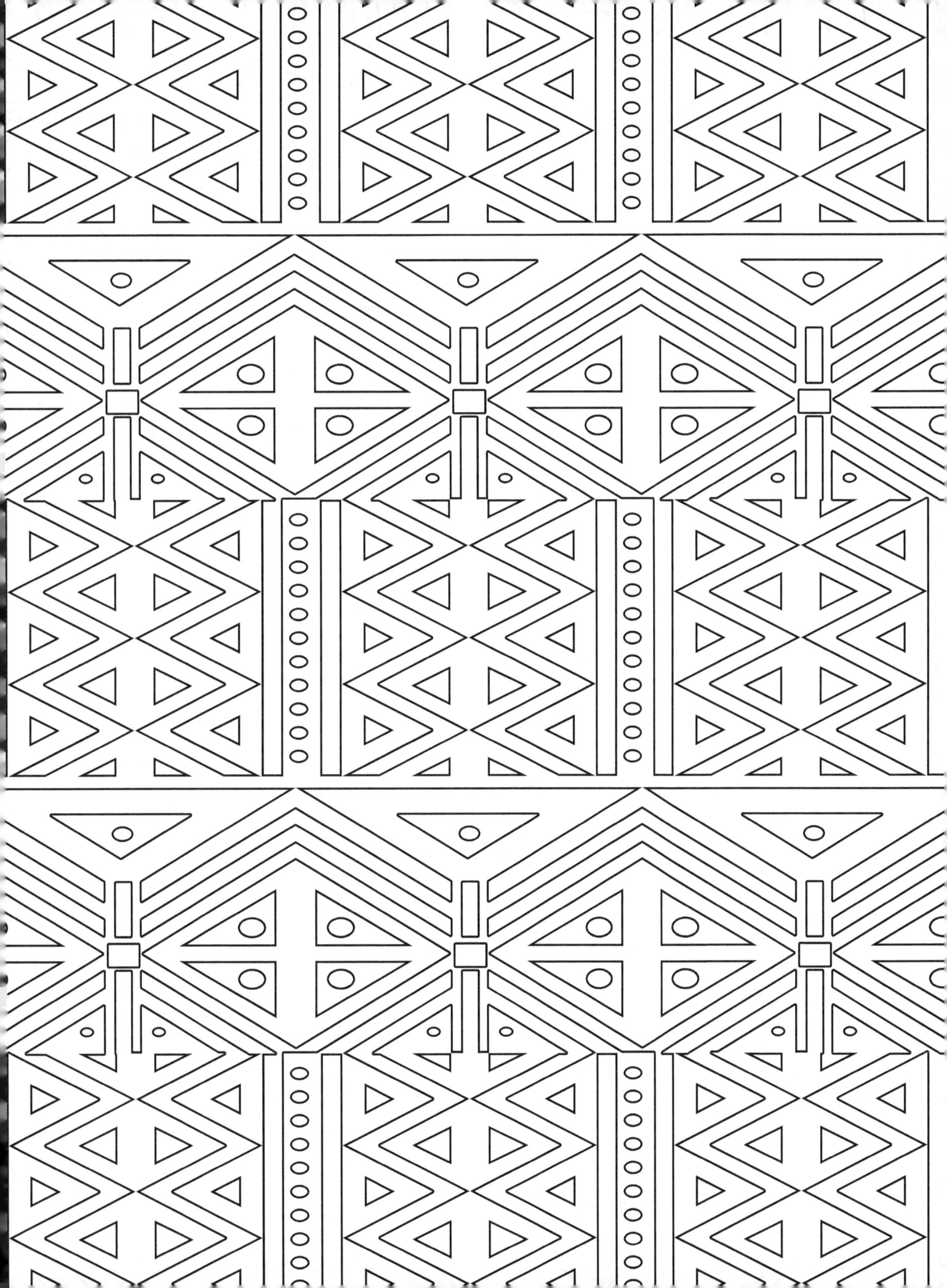

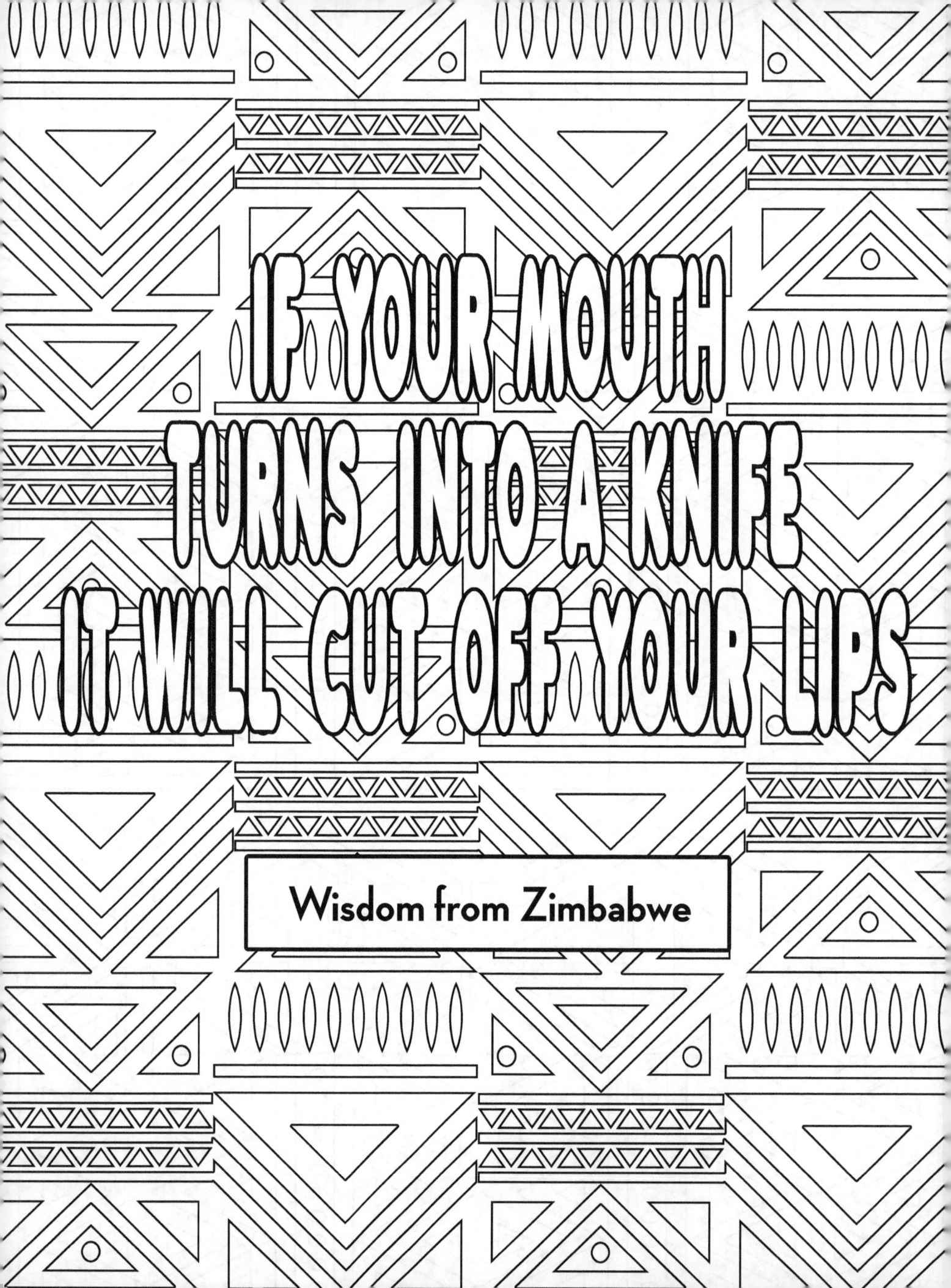

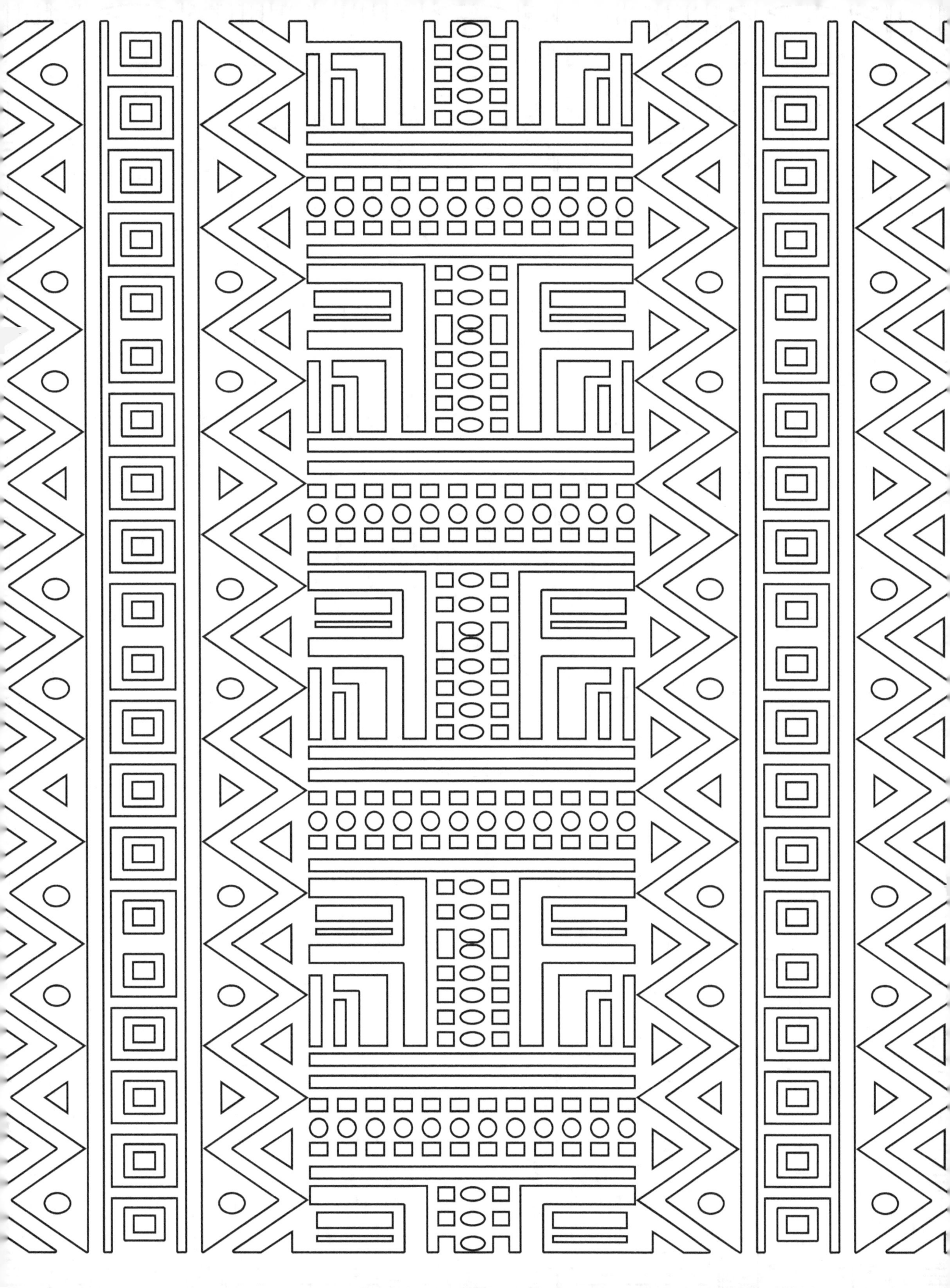

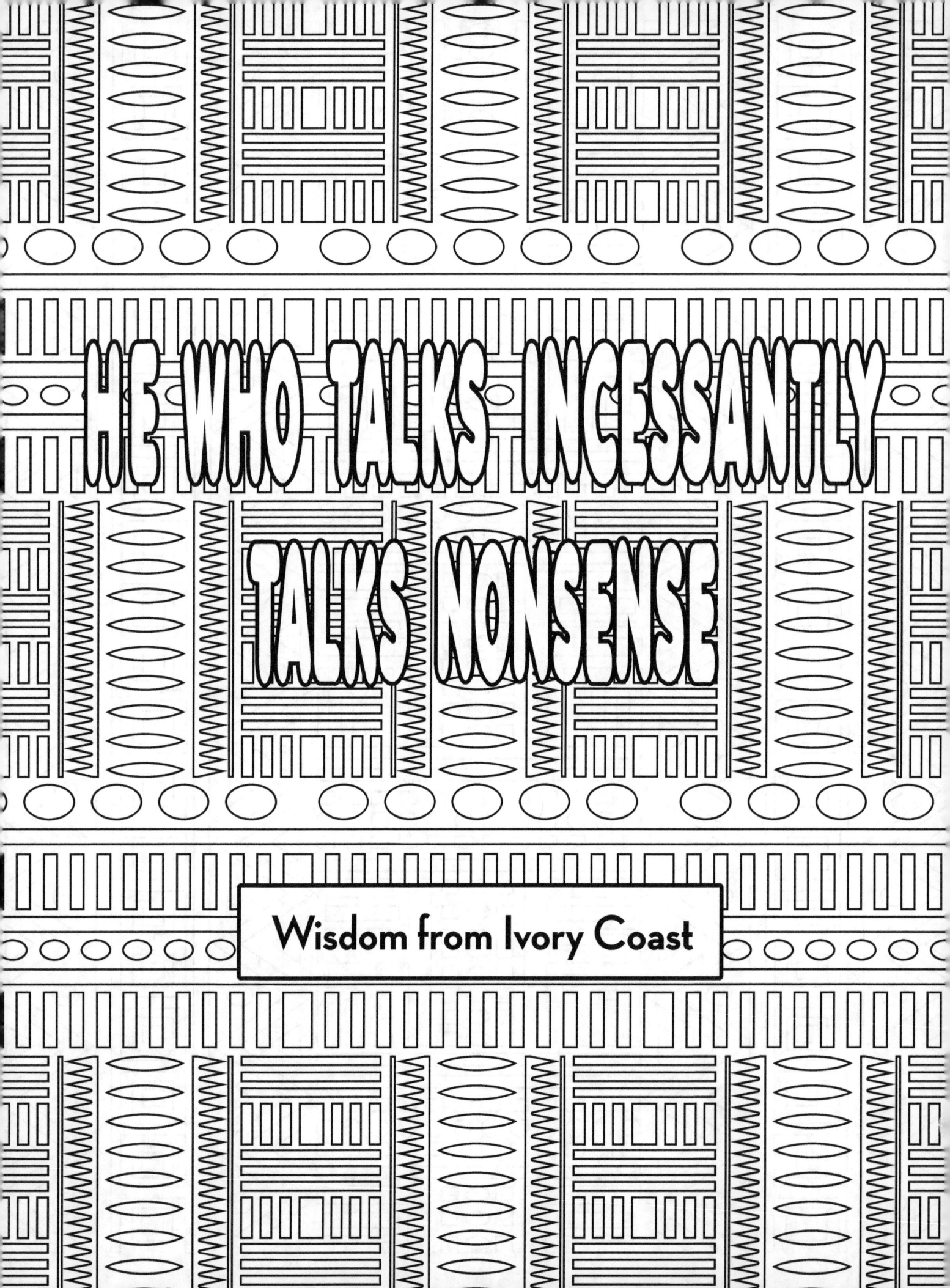

HE WHO TALKS INCESSANTLY TALKS NONSENSE

Wisdom from Ivory Coast

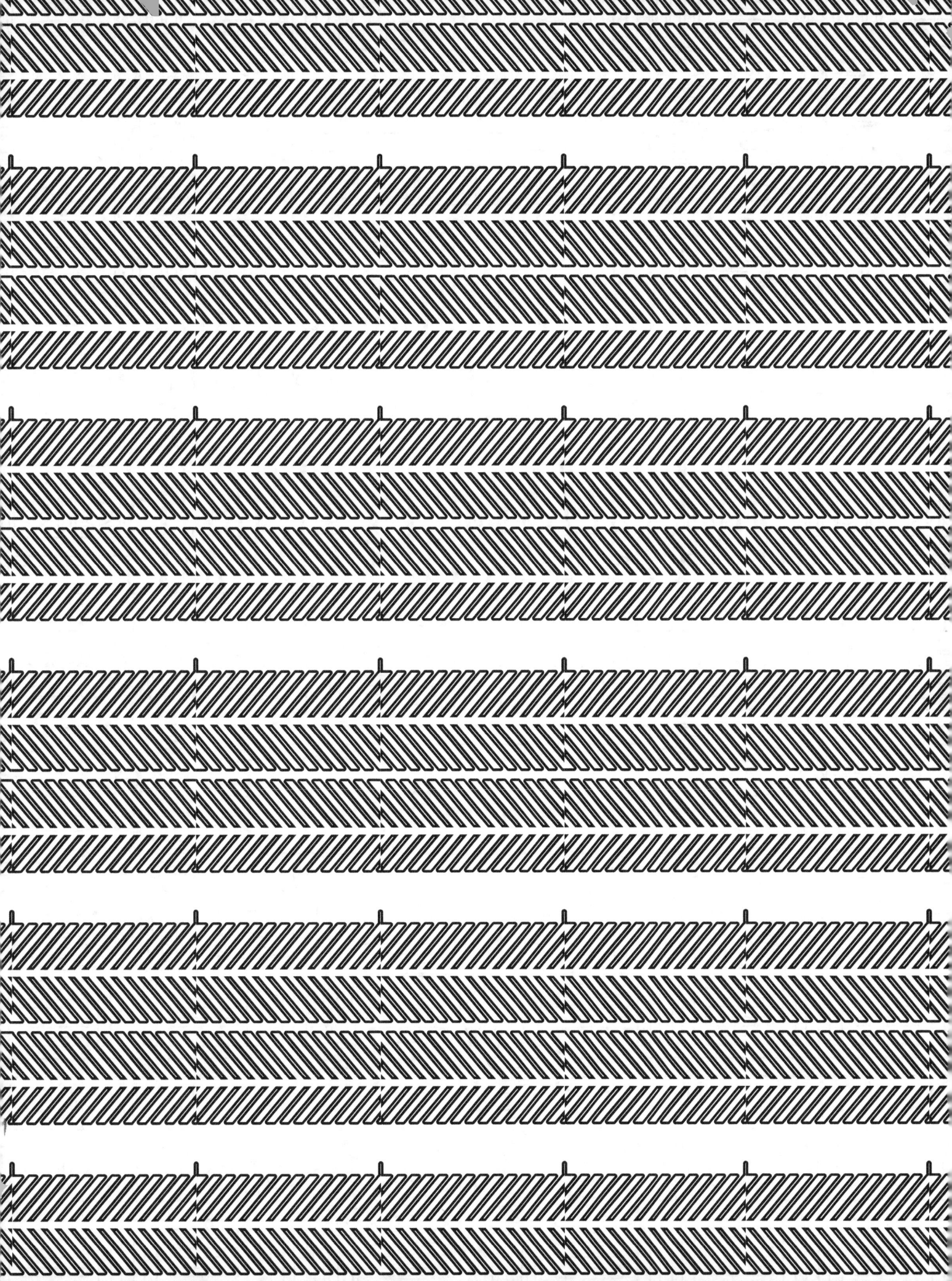

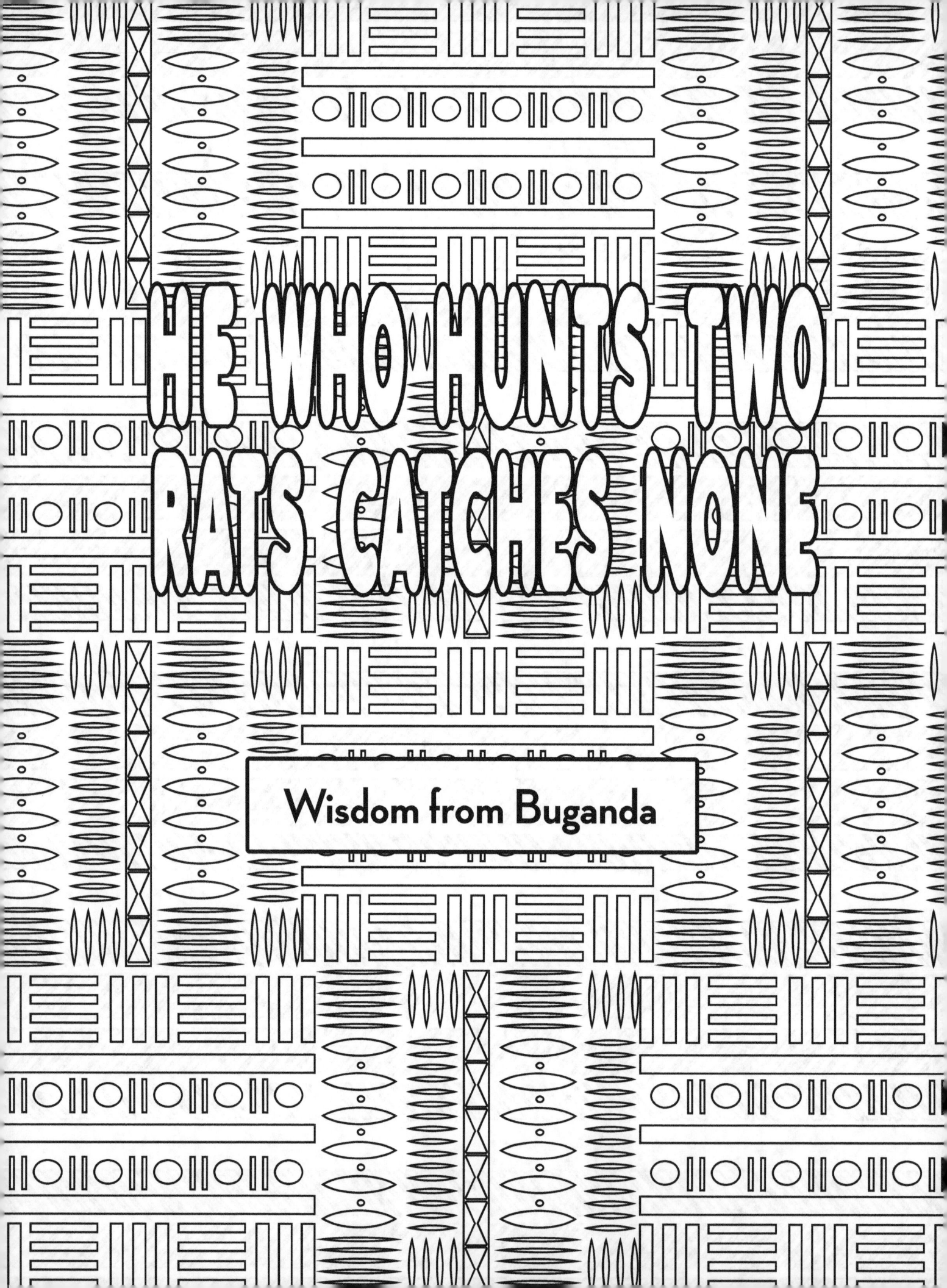

HE WHO HUNTS TWO RATS CATCHES NONE

Wisdom from Buganda

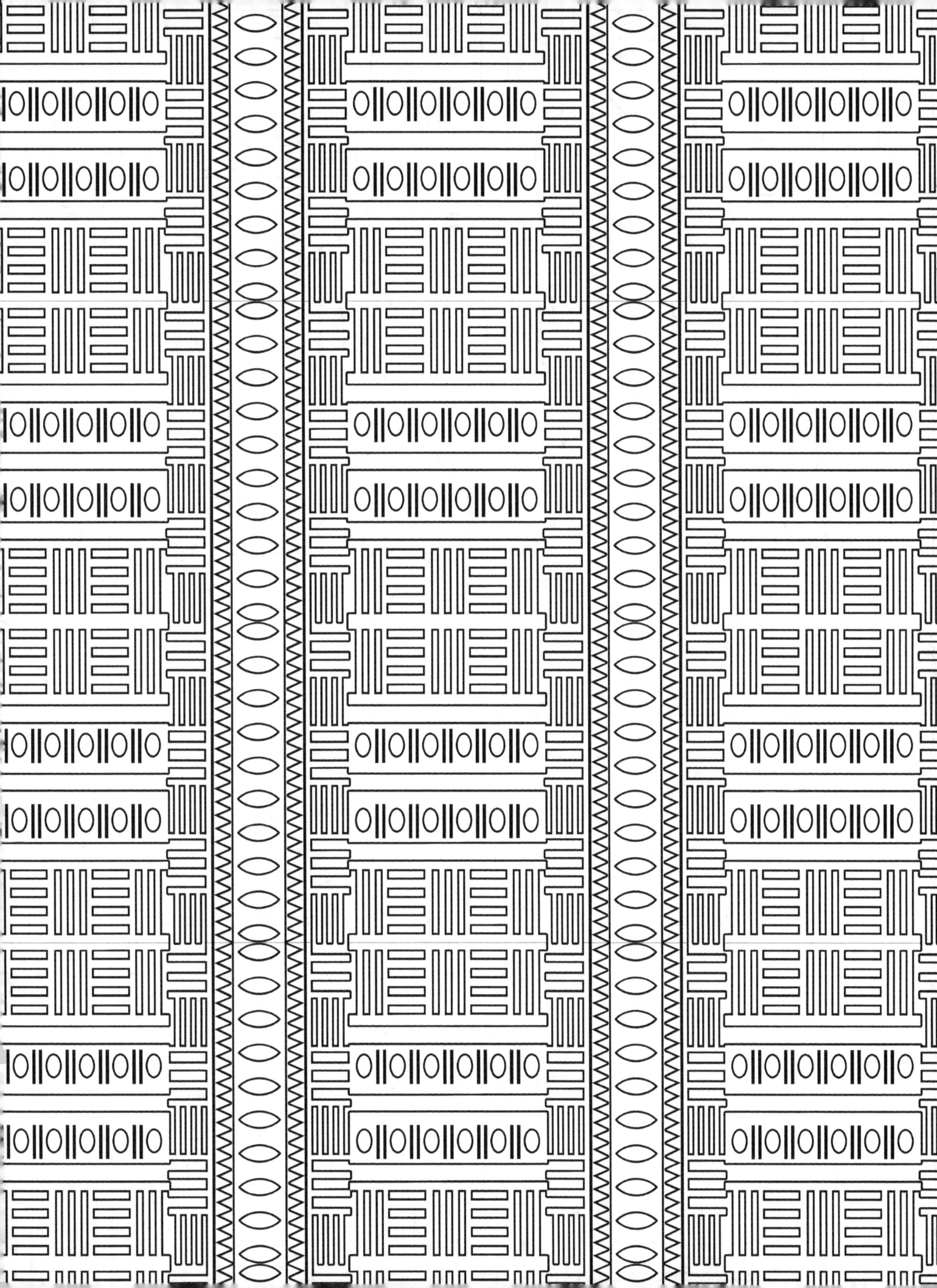

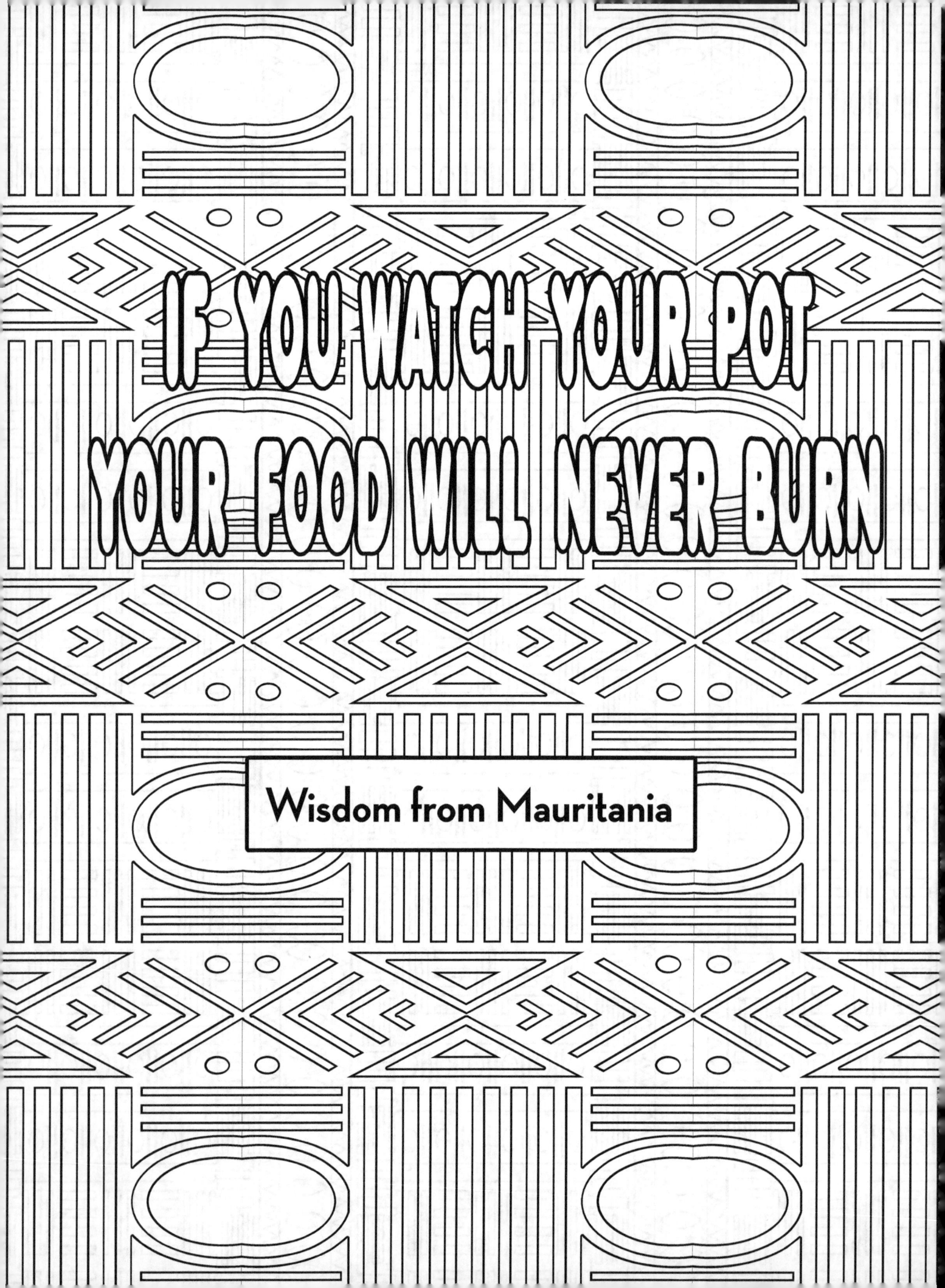

IF YOU WATCH YOUR POT YOUR FOOD WILL NEVER BURN

Wisdom from Mauritania

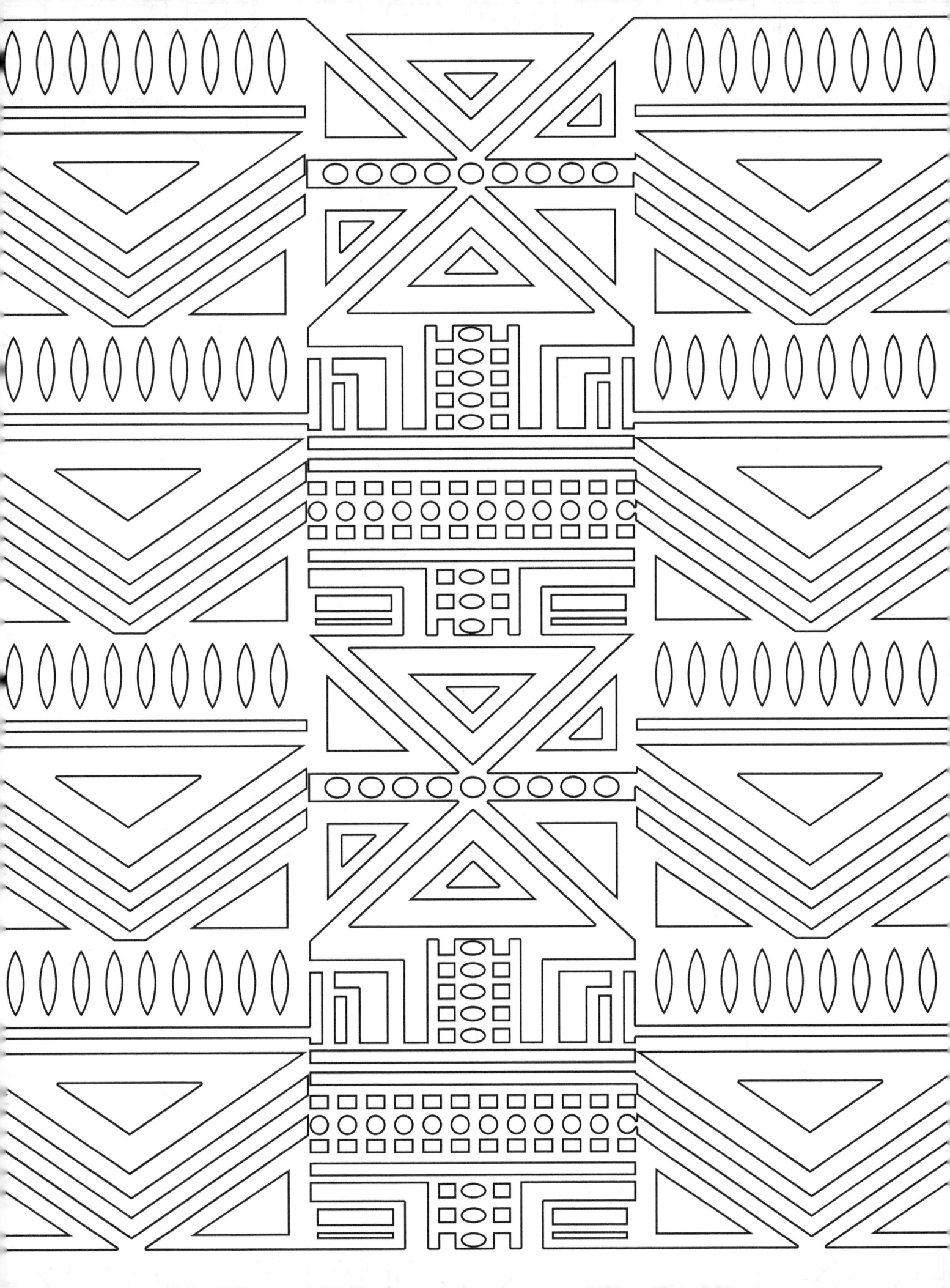

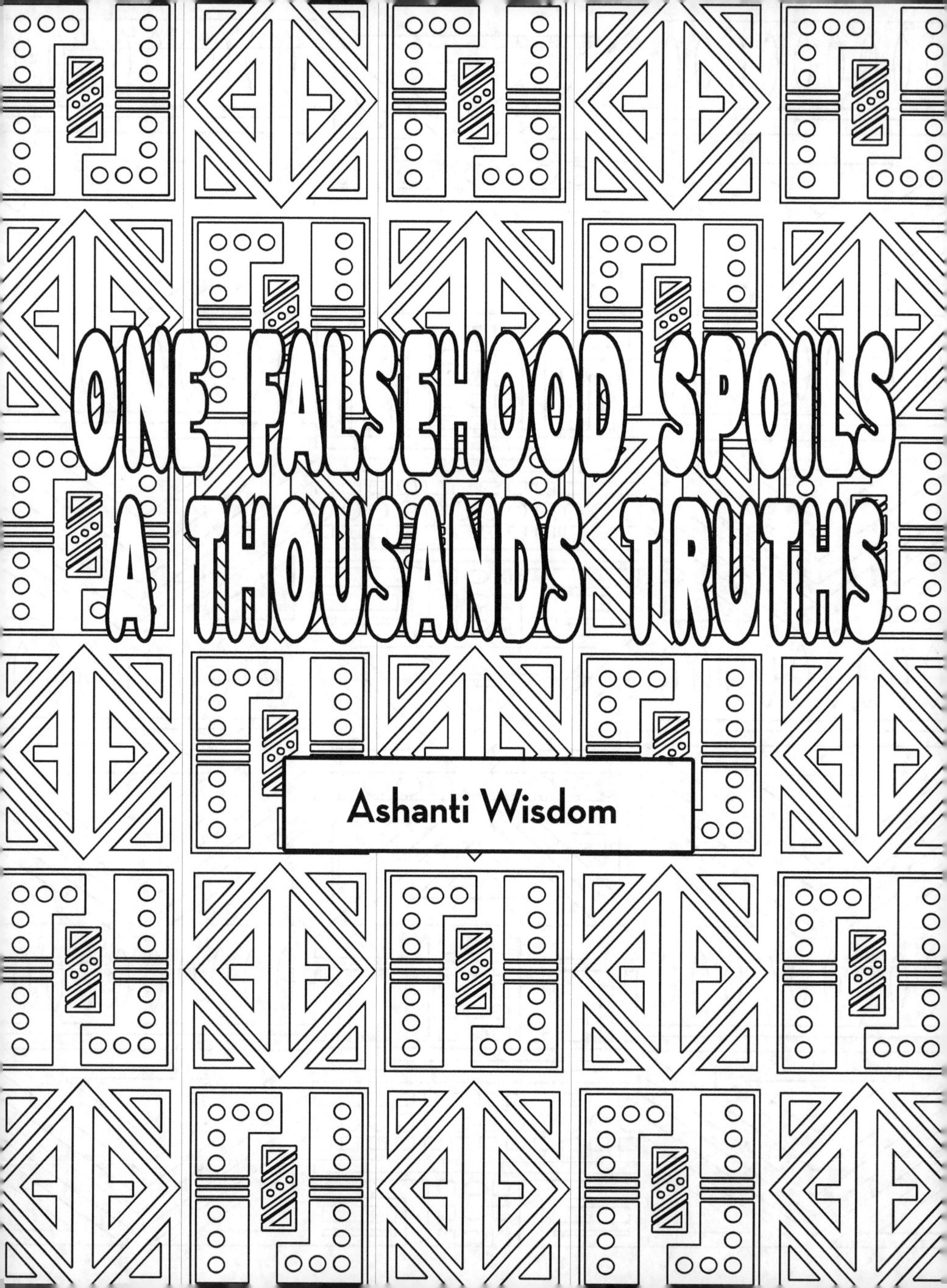

ONE FALSEHOOD SPOILS A THOUSANDS TRUTHS

Ashanti Wisdom

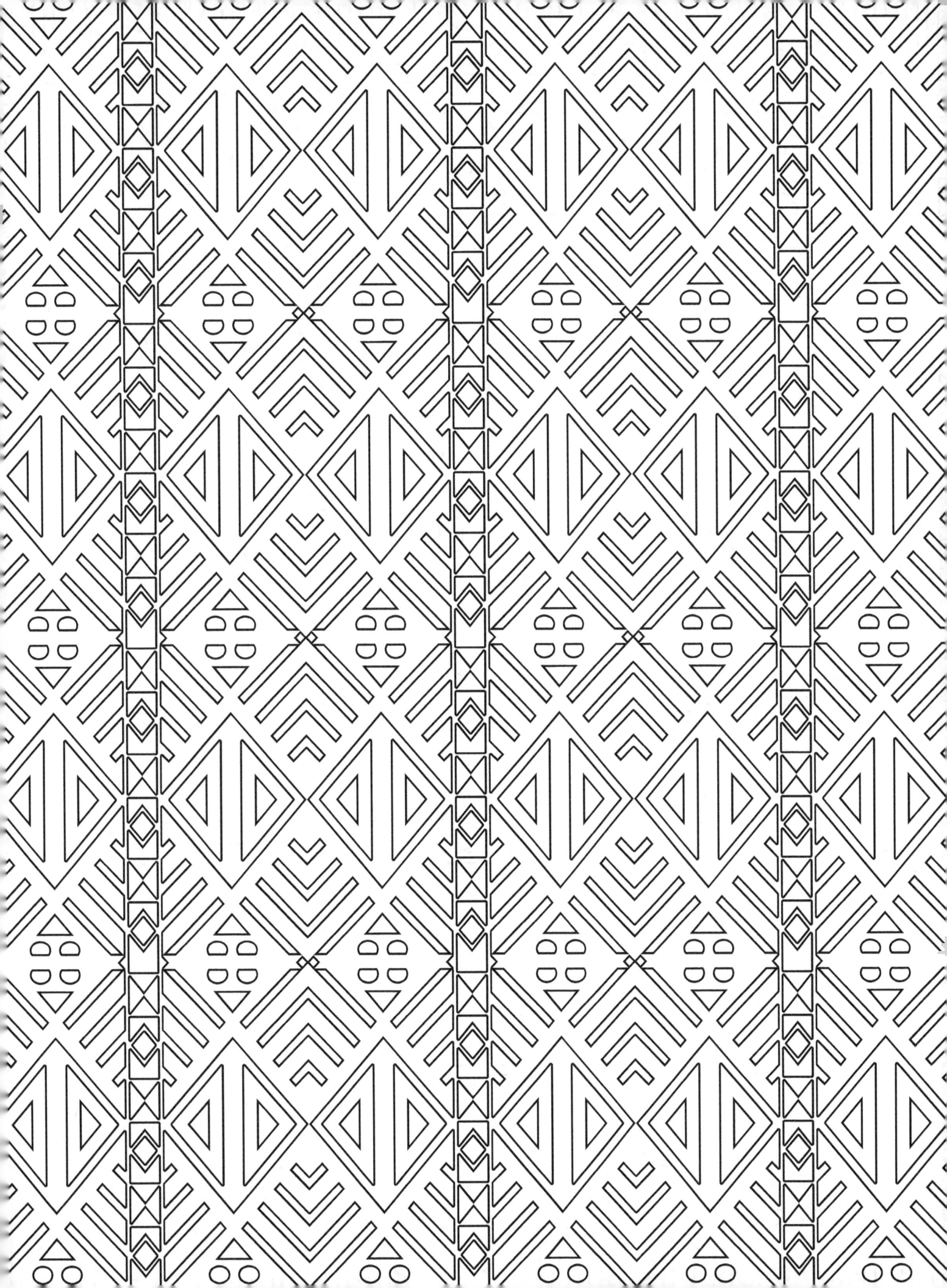

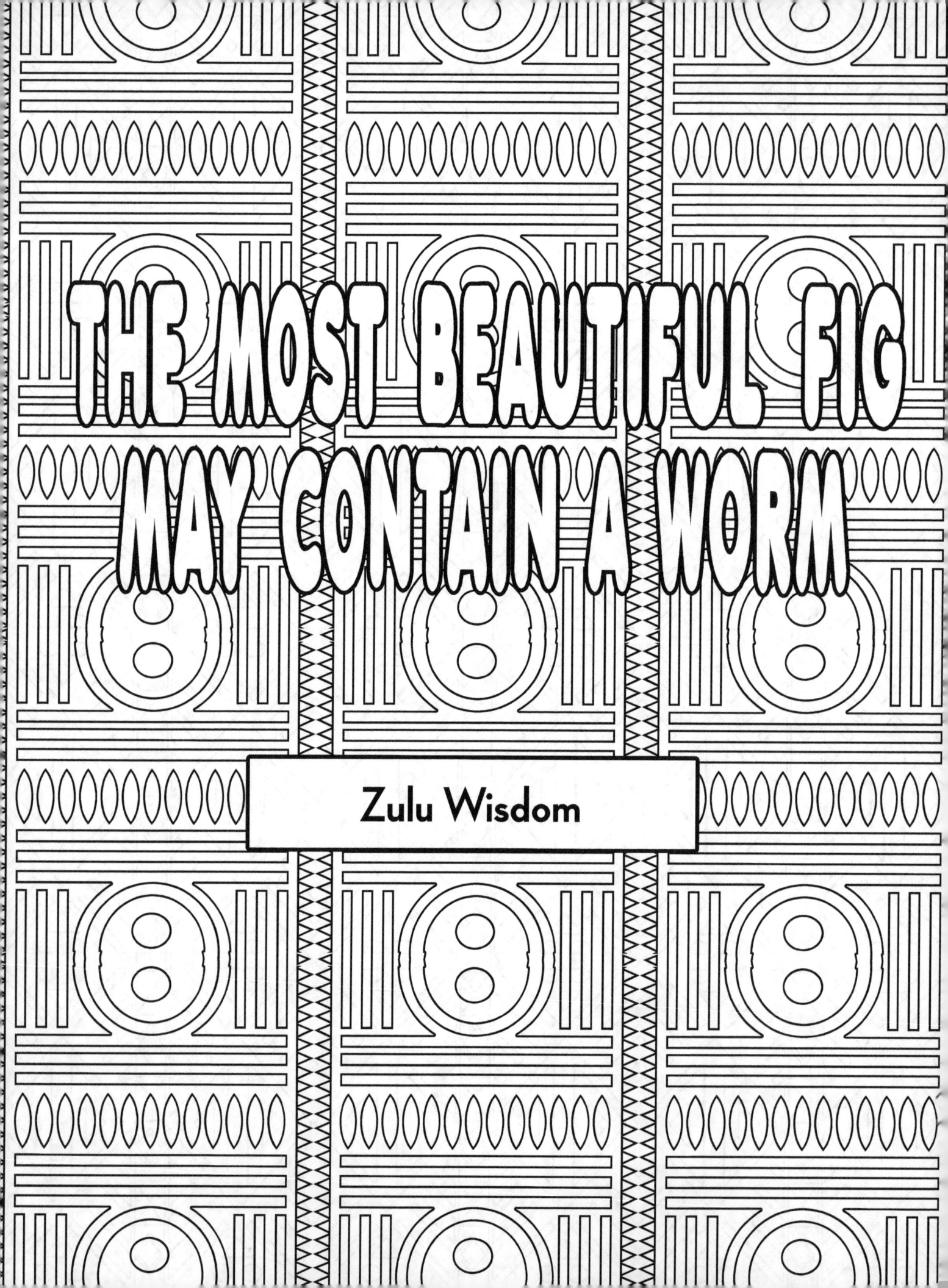

THE MOST BEAUTIFUL FIG
MAY CONTAIN A WORM

Zulu Wisdom

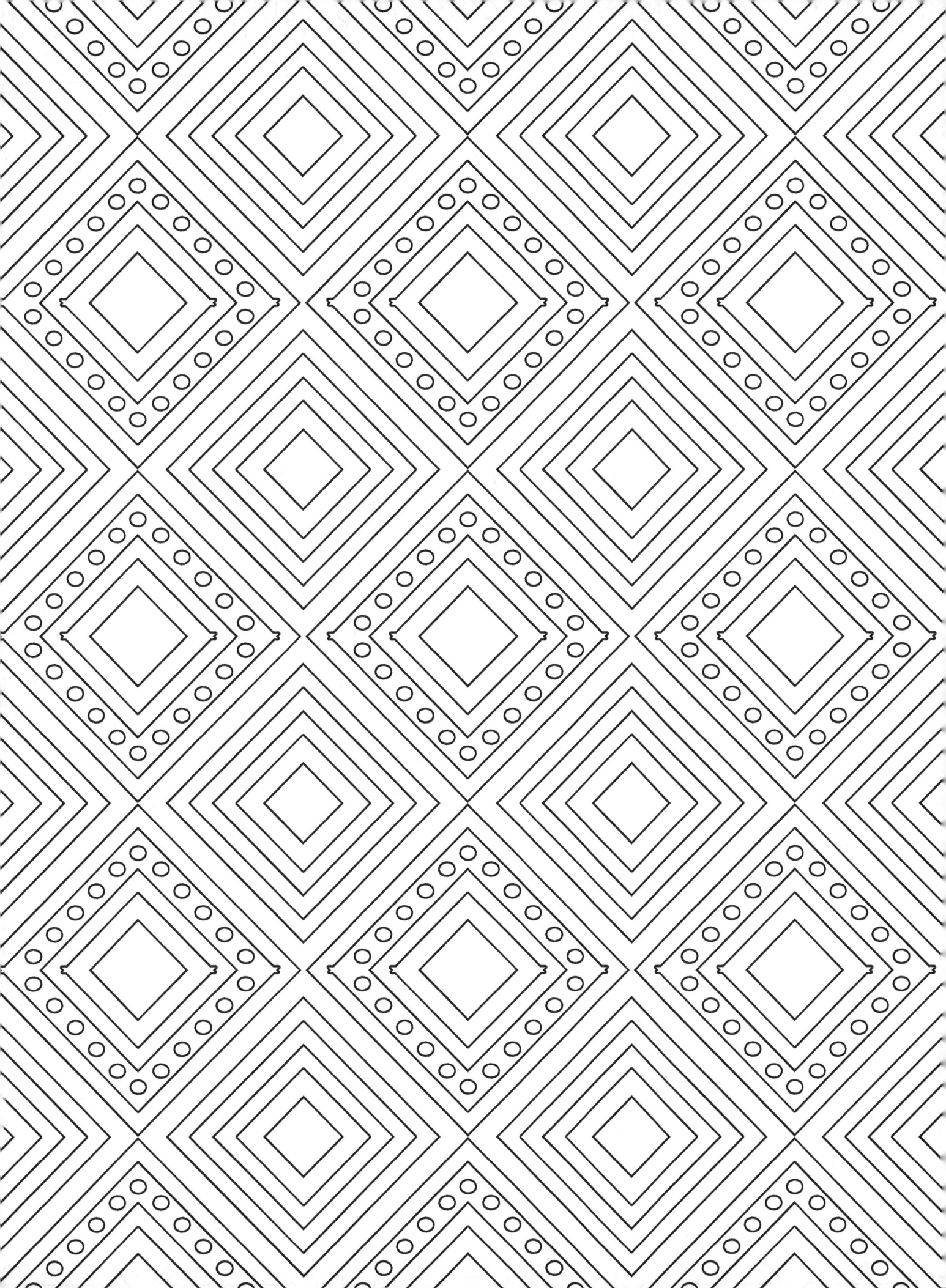

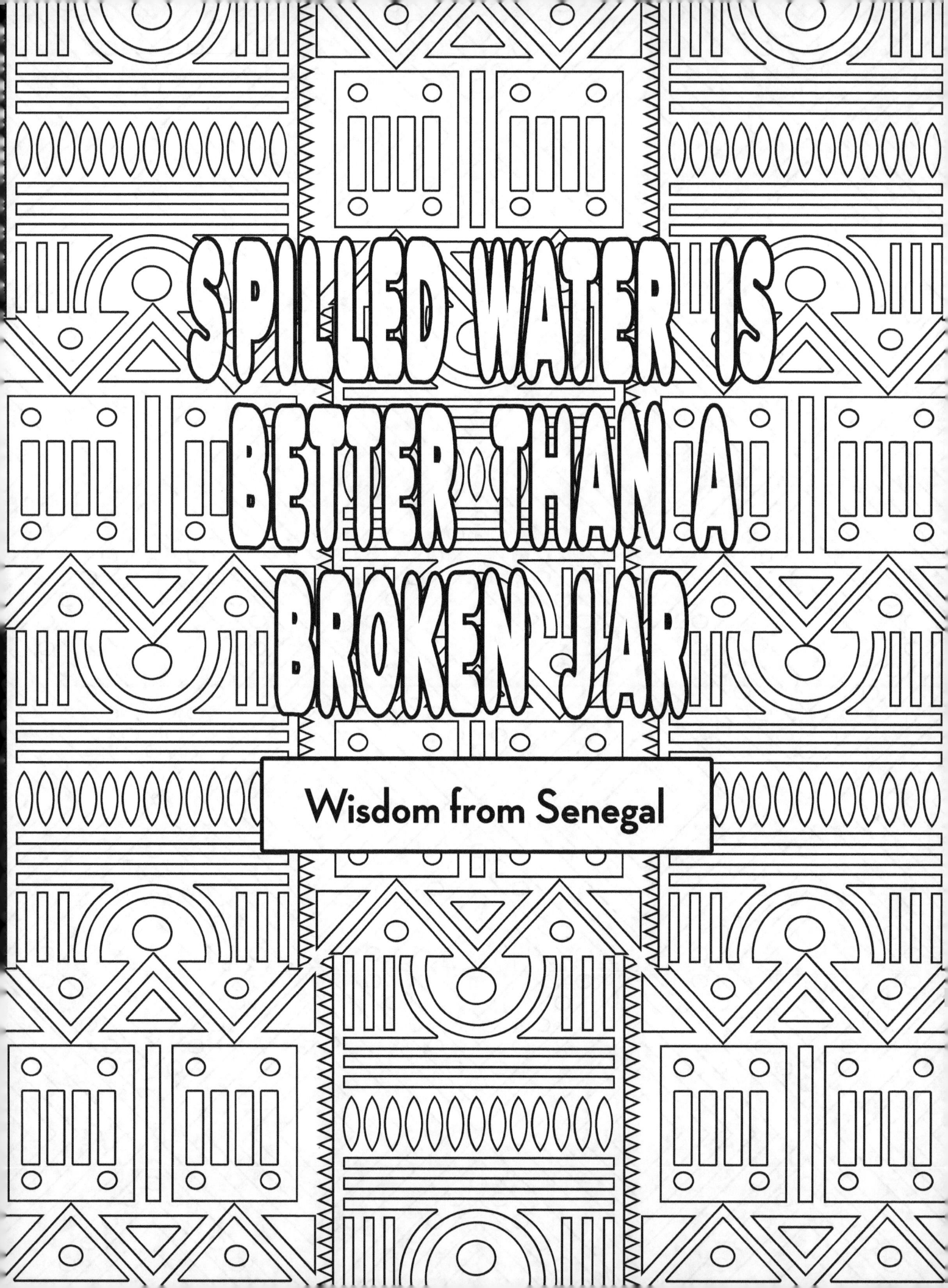

SPILLED WATER IS BETTER THAN A BROKEN JAR

Wisdom from Senegal

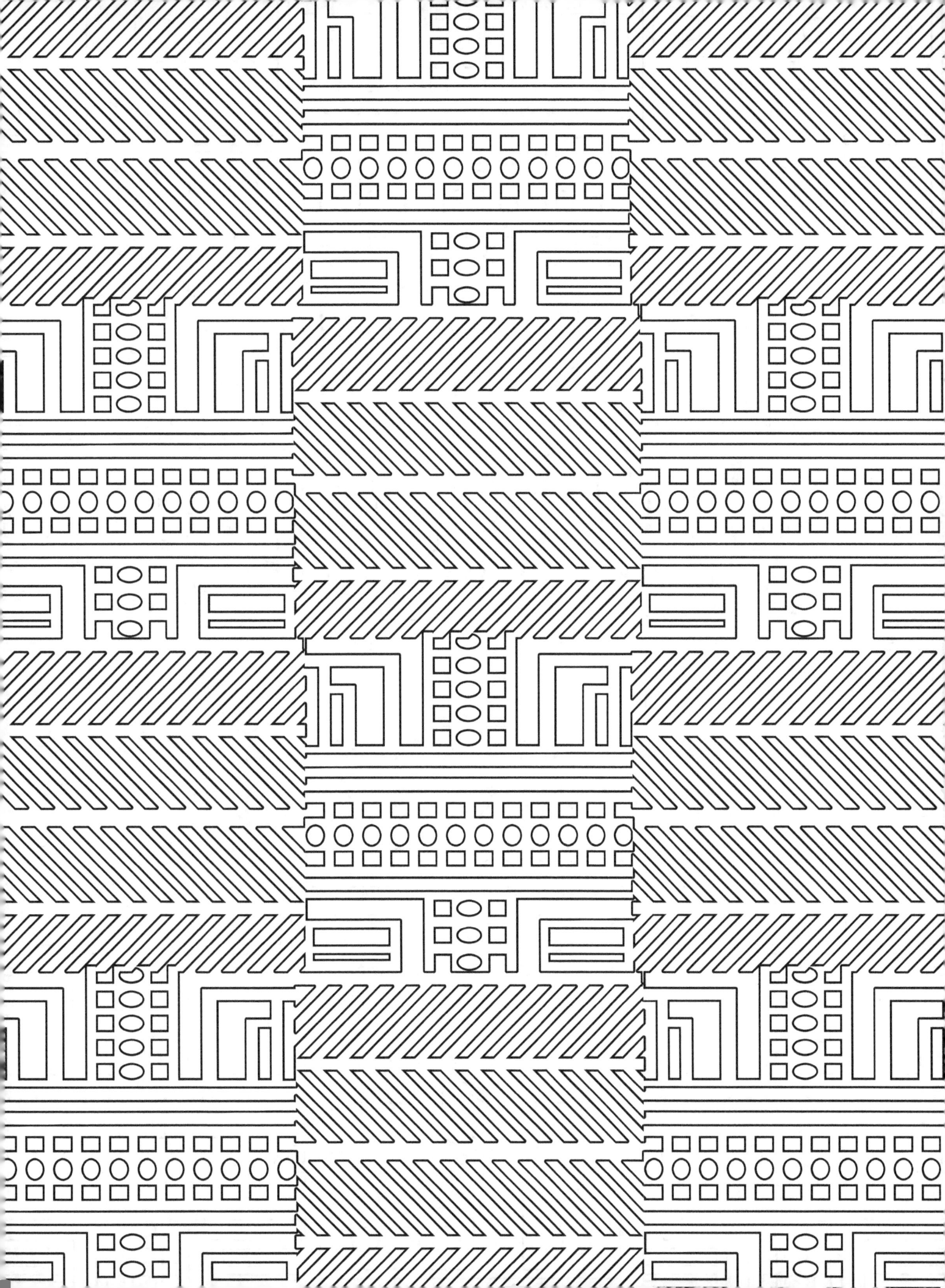

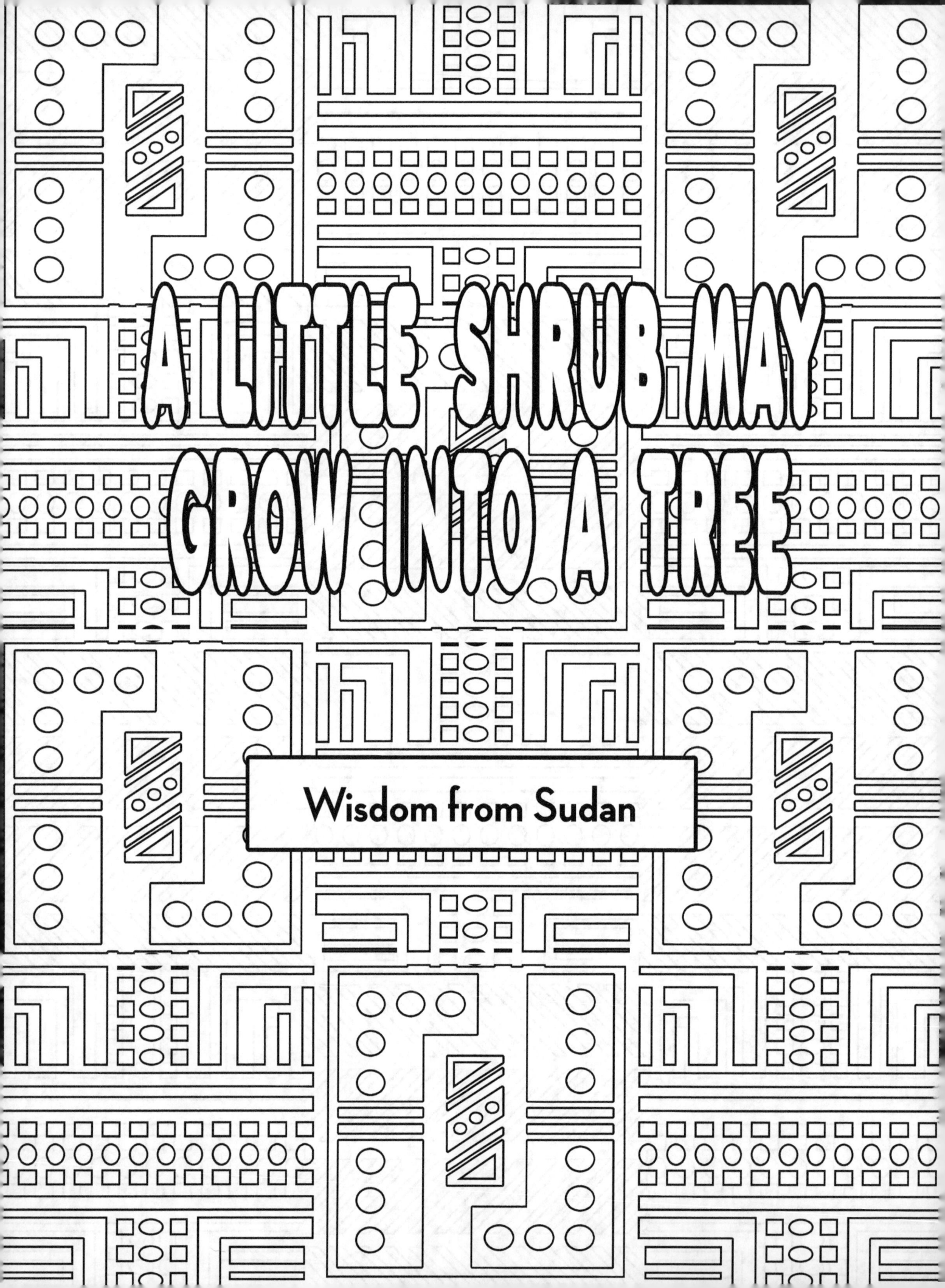

A LITTLE SHRUB MAY GROW INTO A TREE

Wisdom from Sudan

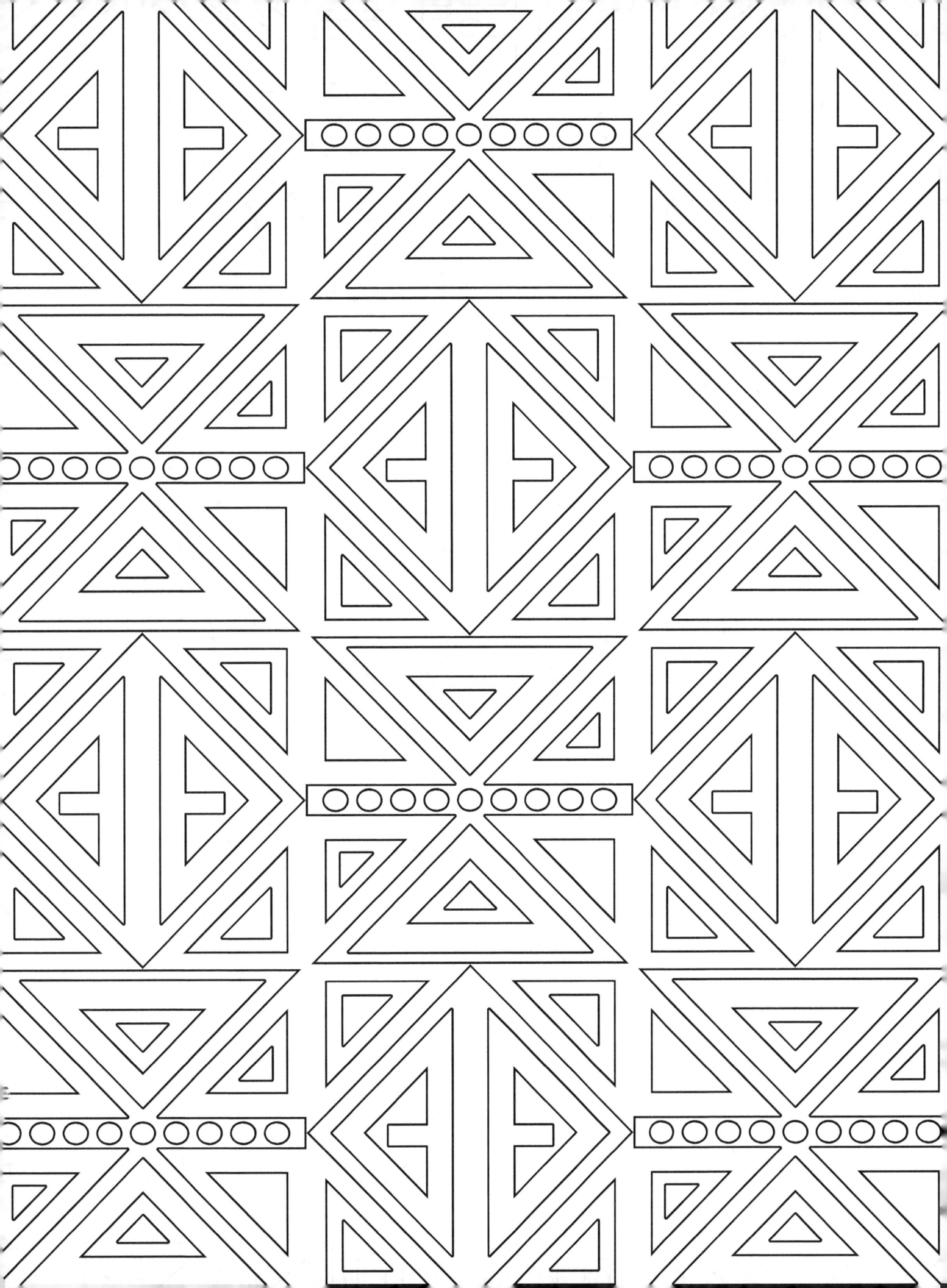

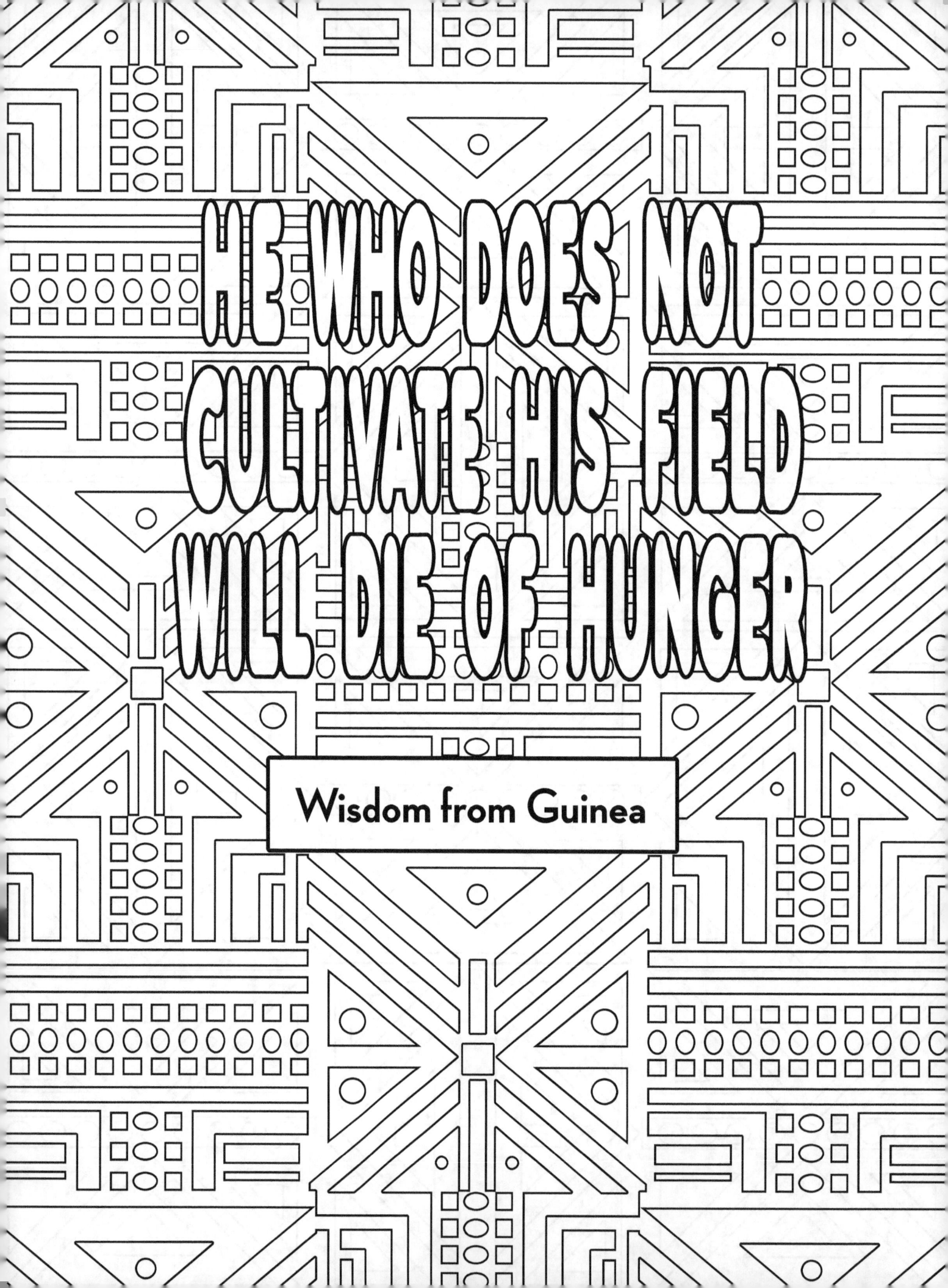

HE WHO DOES NOT CULTIVATE HIS FIELD WILL DIE OF HUNGER

Wisdom from Guinea

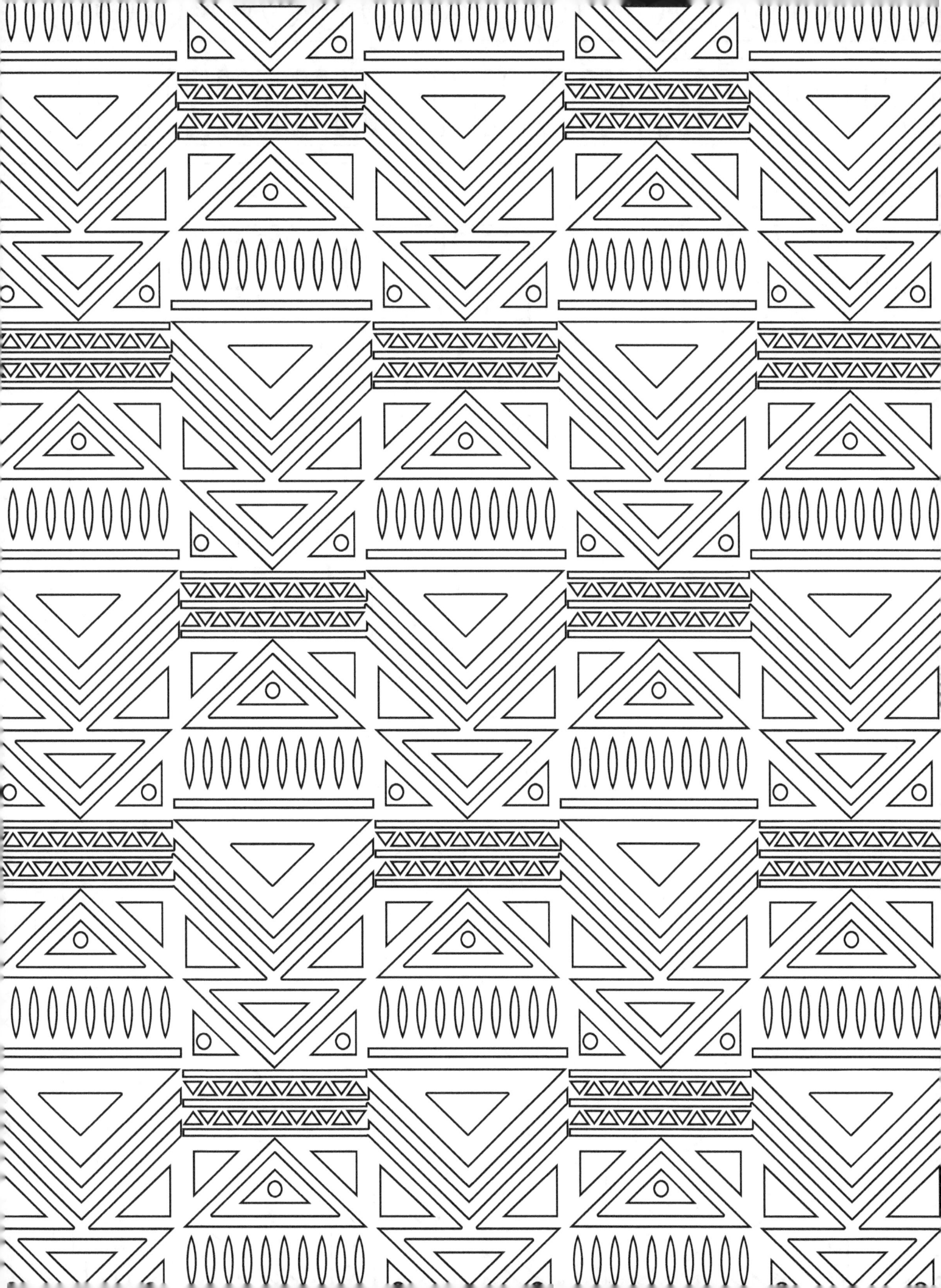

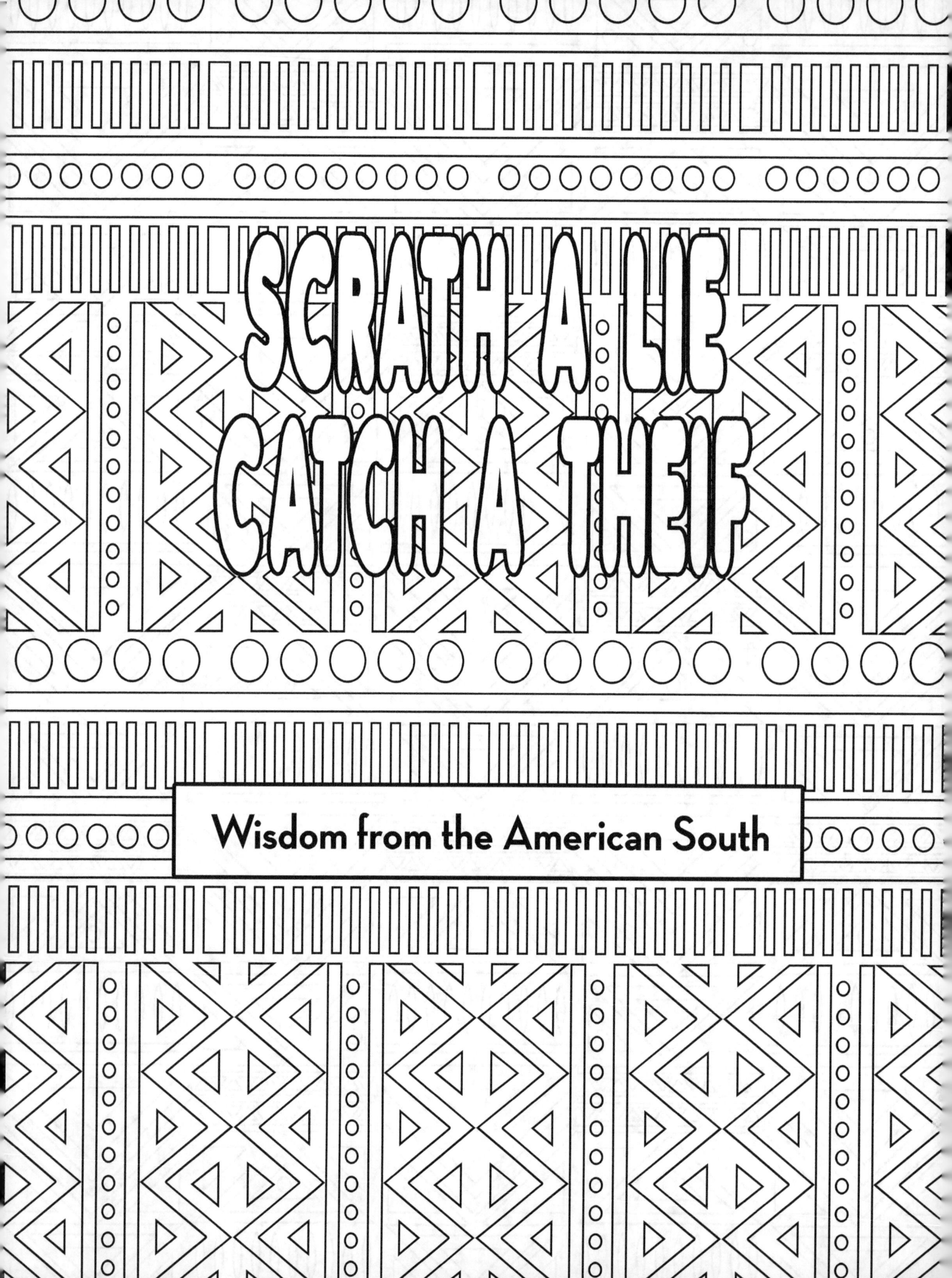

SCRATH A LIE CATCH A THEIF

Wisdom from the American South

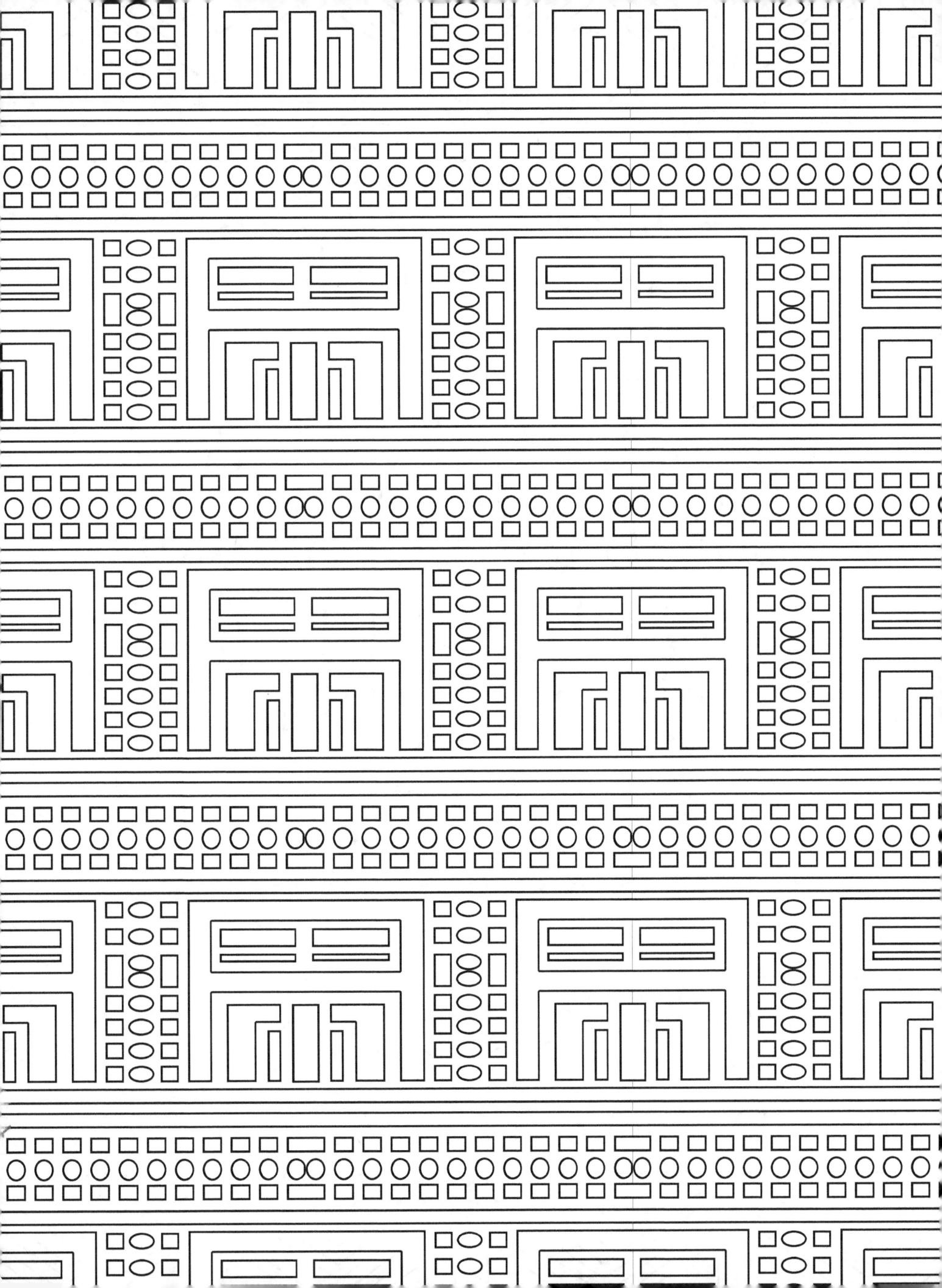

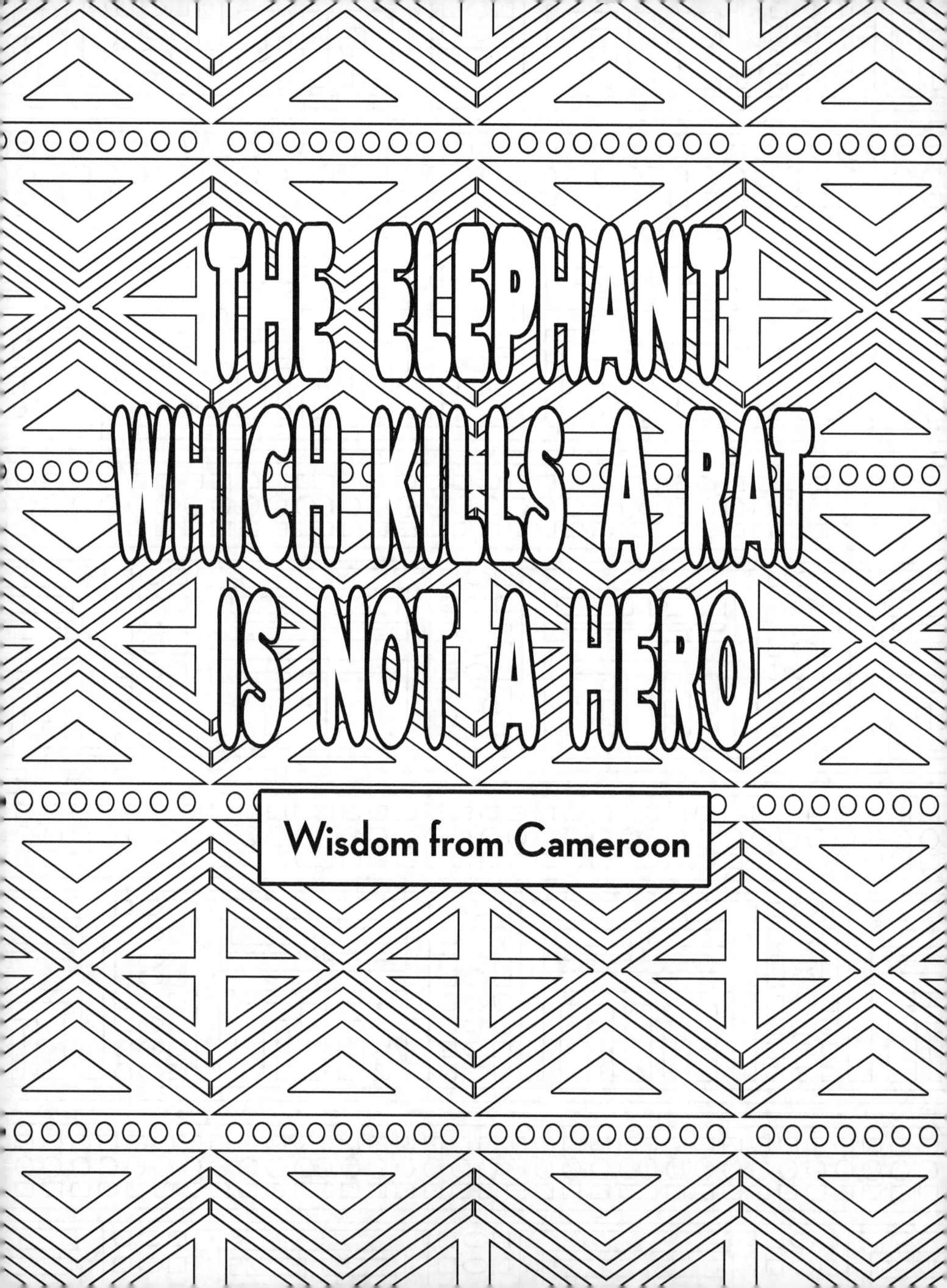

THE ELEPHANT WHICH KILLS A RAT IS NOT A HERO

Wisdom from Cameroon

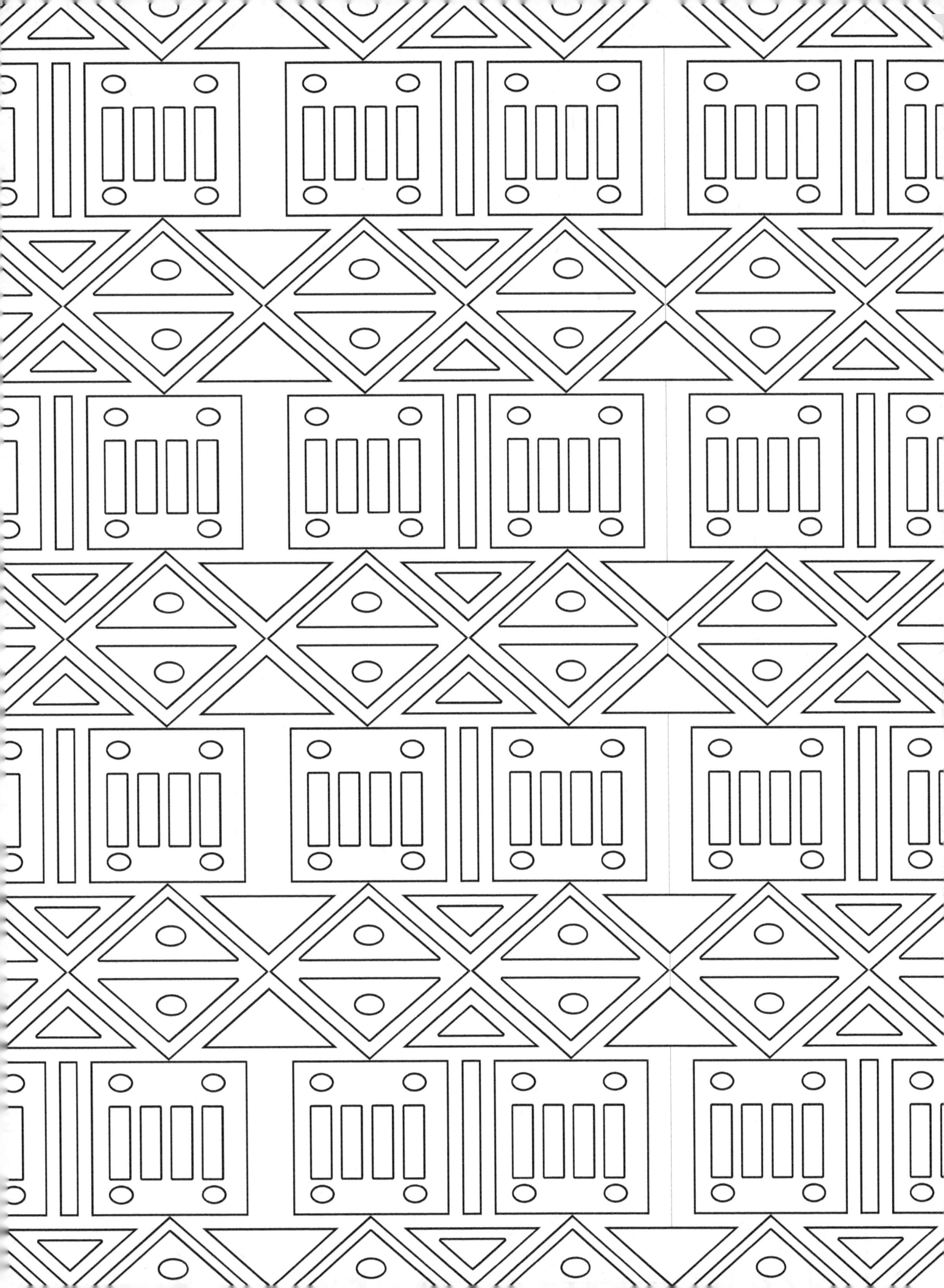

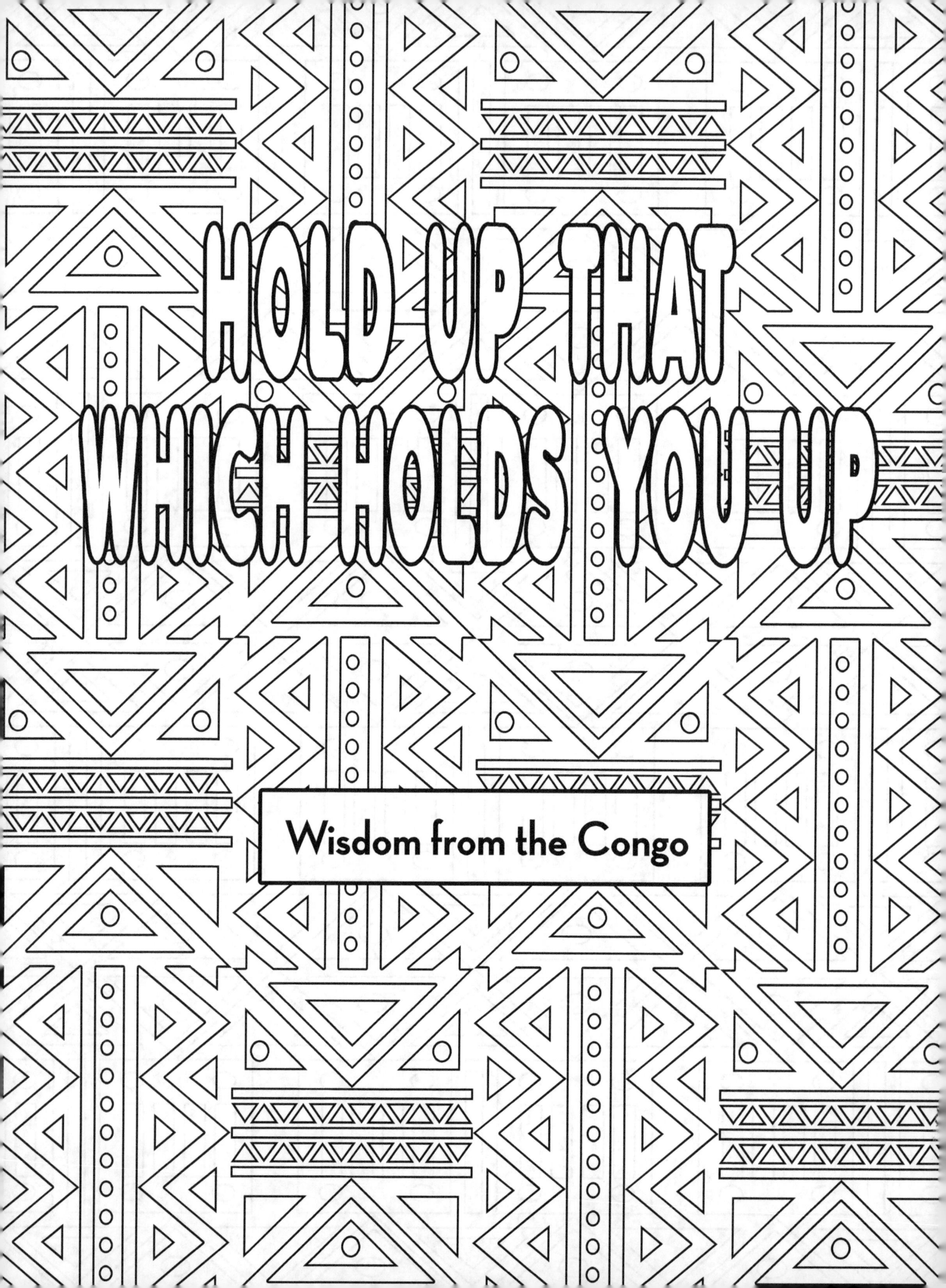

HOLD UP THAT WHICH HOLDS YOU UP

Wisdom from the Congo

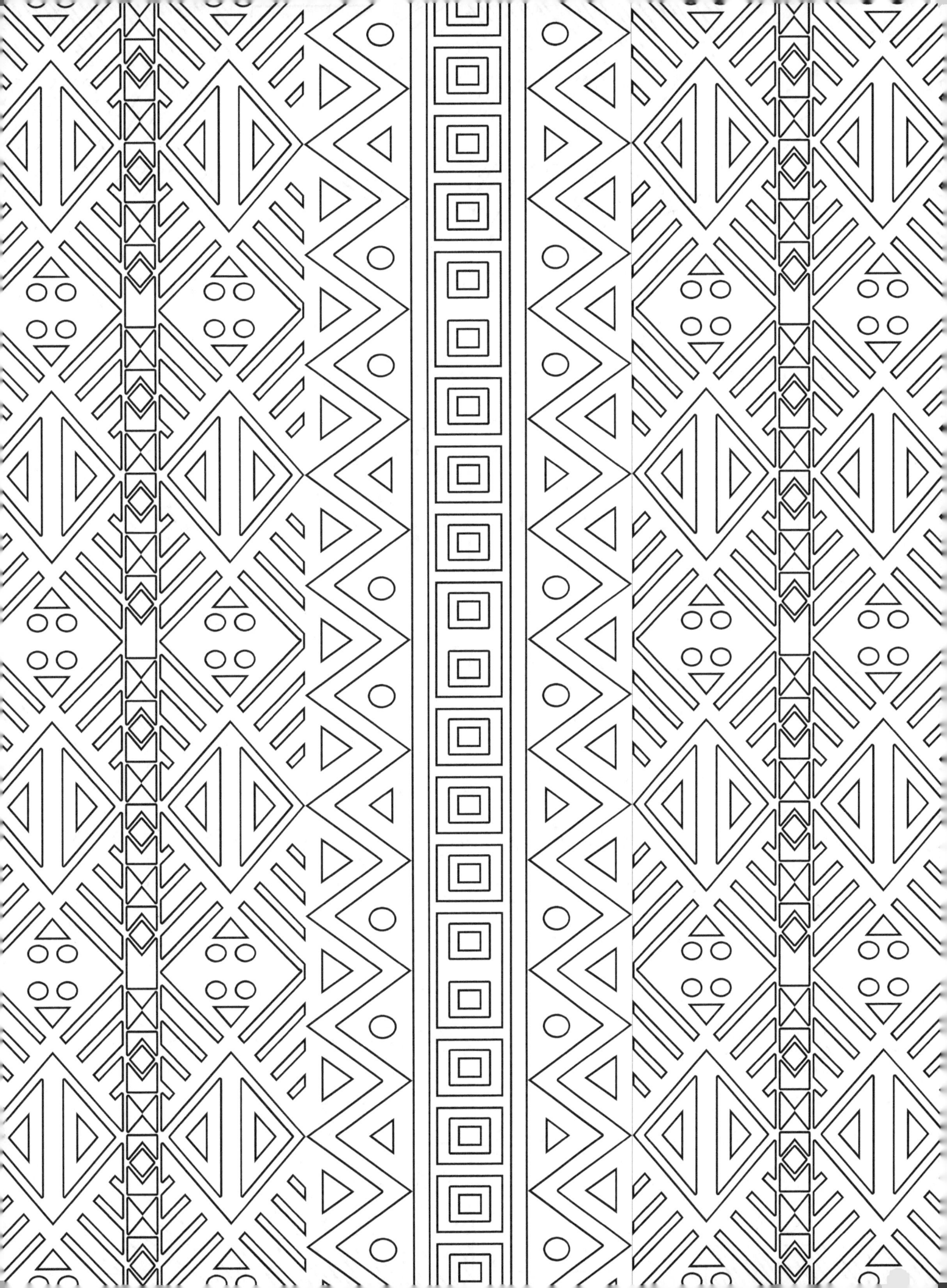

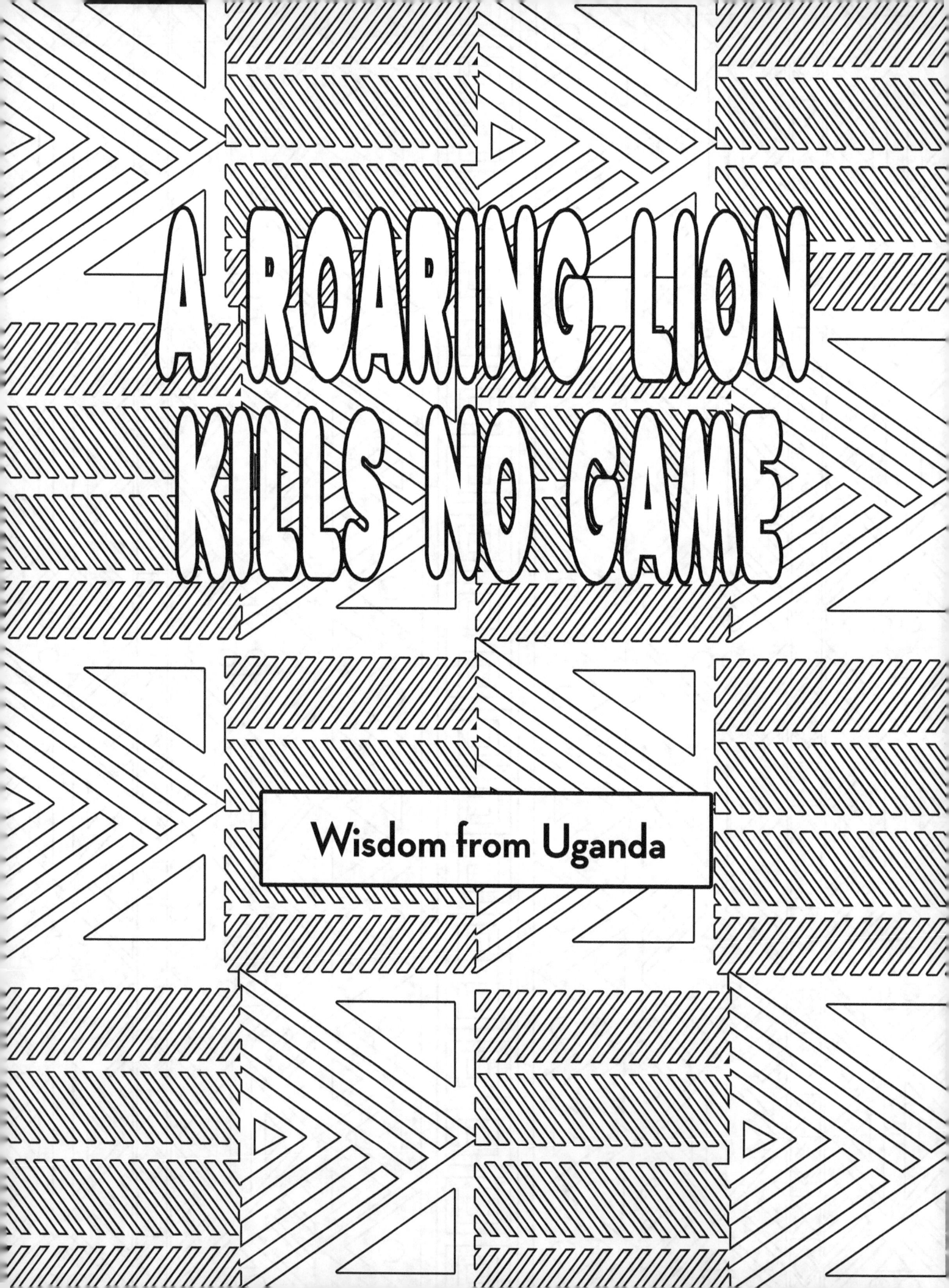

A ROARING LION KILLS NO GAME

Wisdom from Uganda

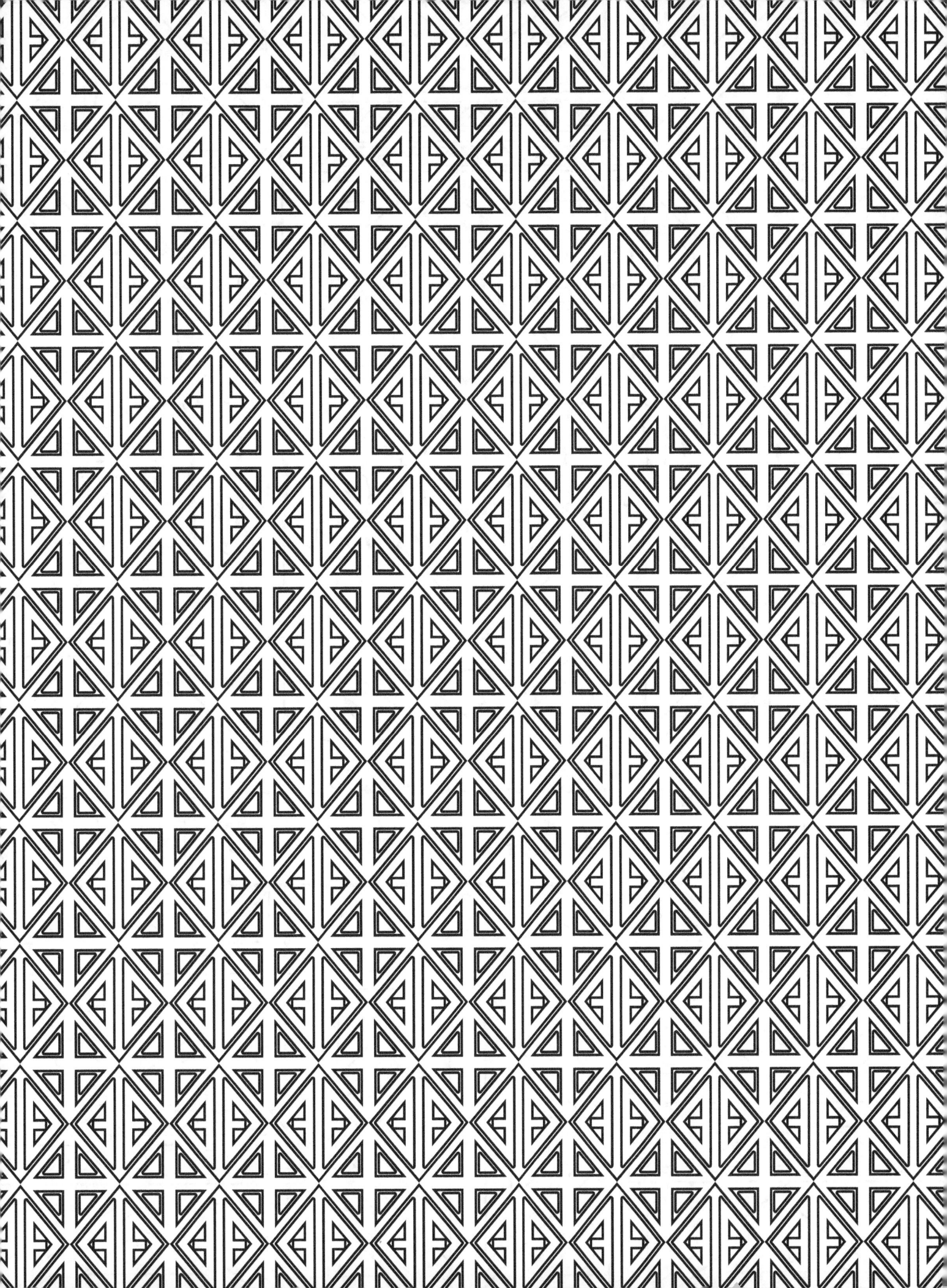

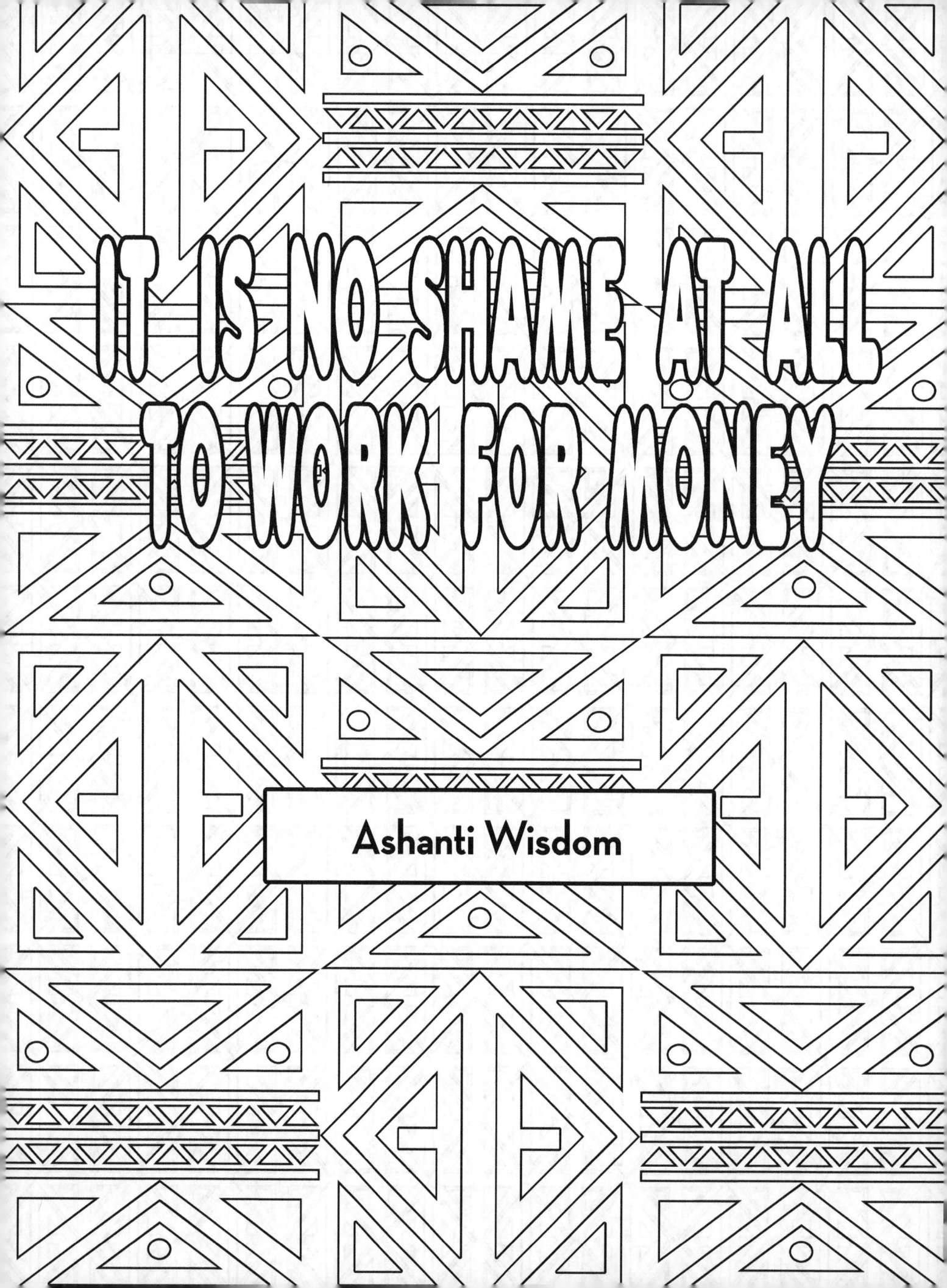

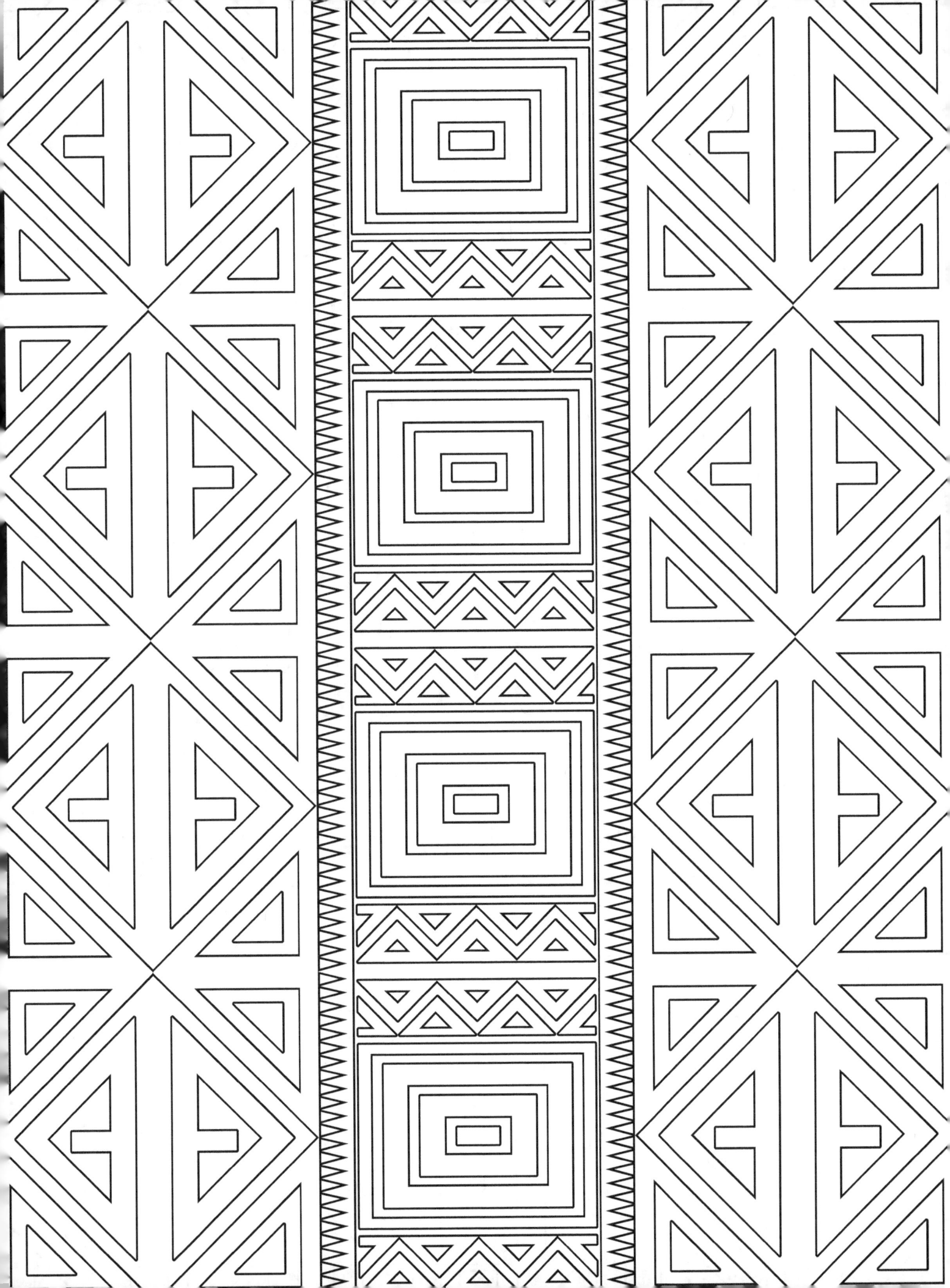

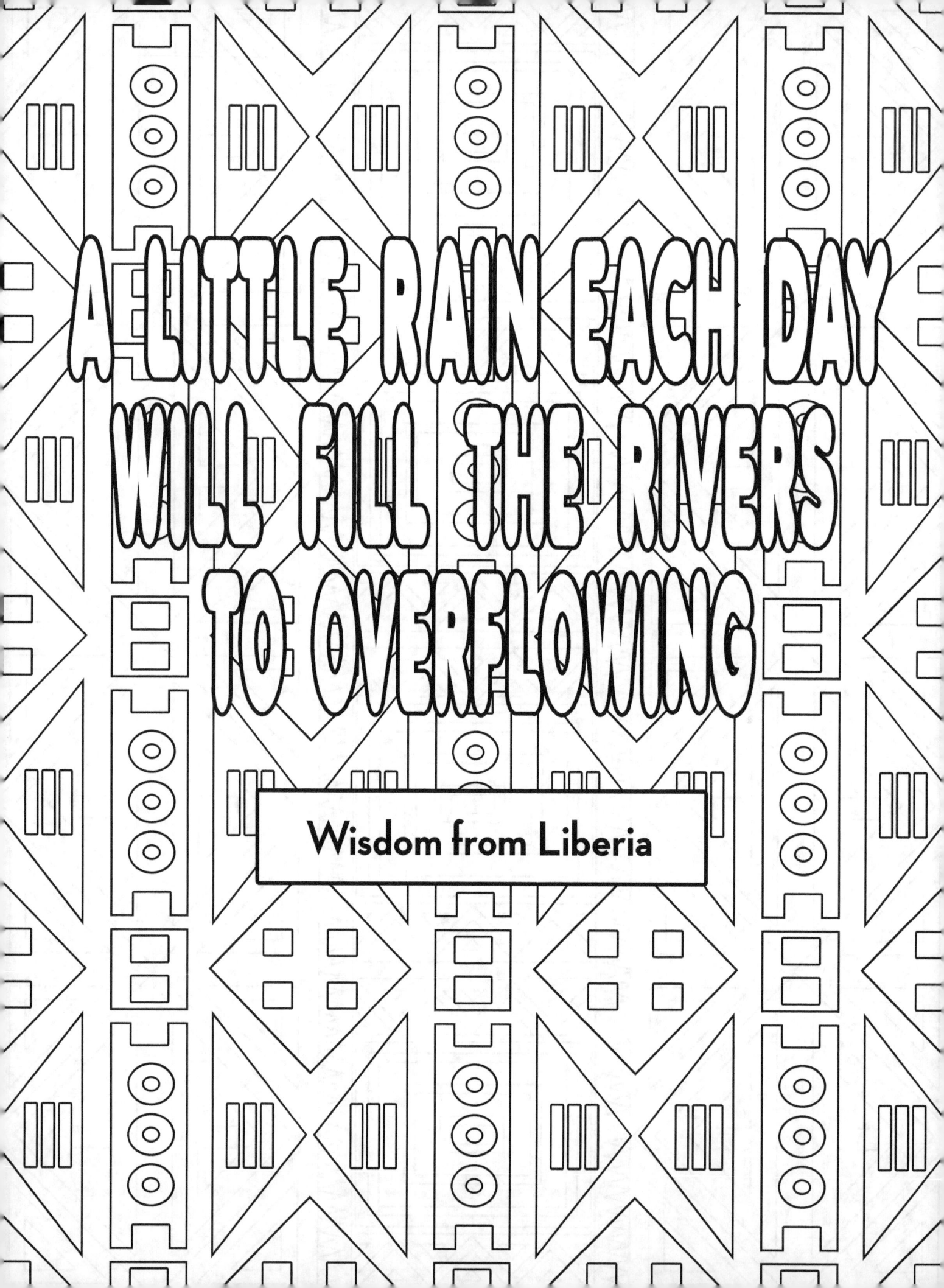

A LITTLE RAIN EACH DAY WILL FILL THE RIVERS TO OVERFLOWING

Wisdom from Liberia

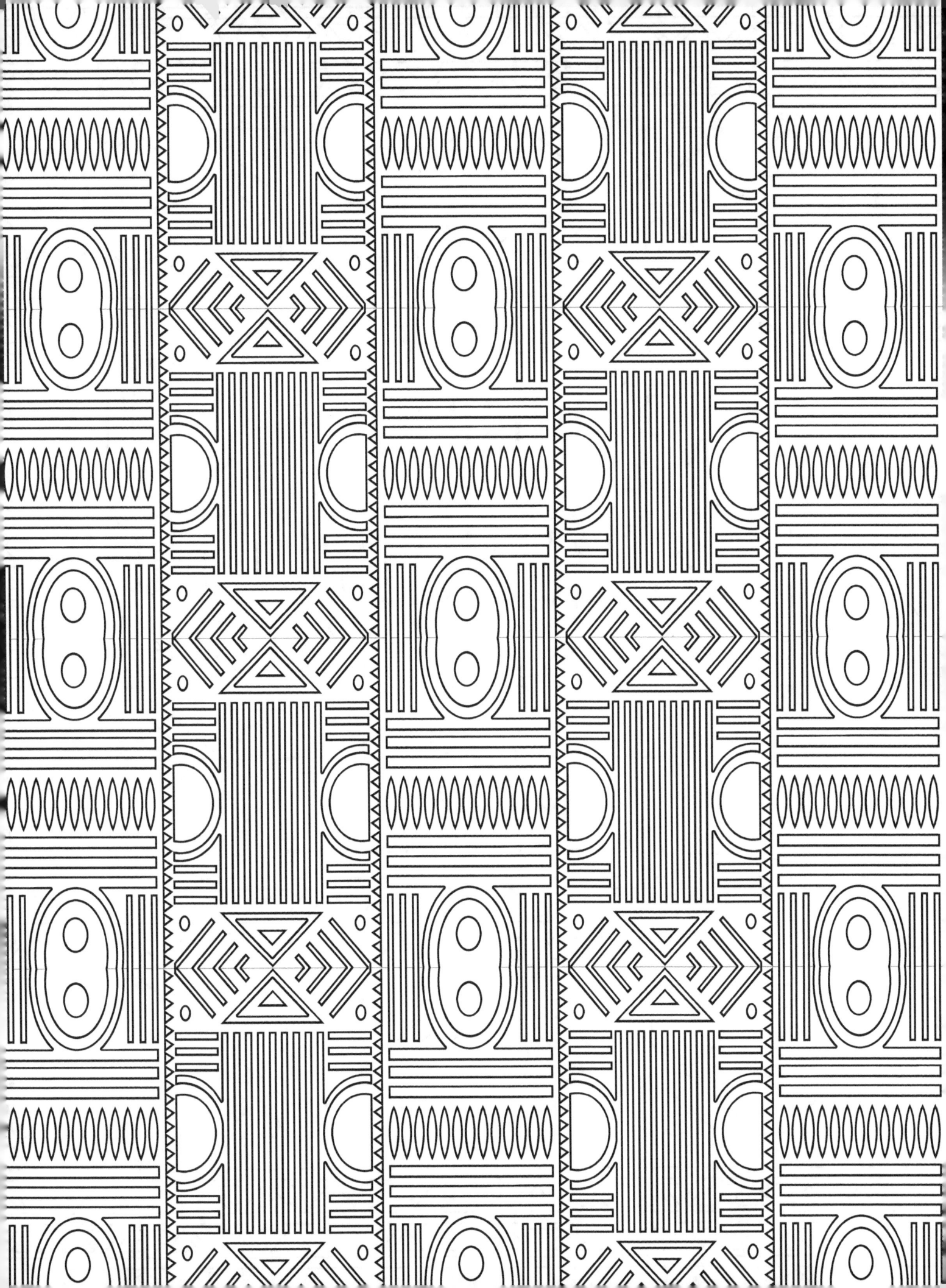

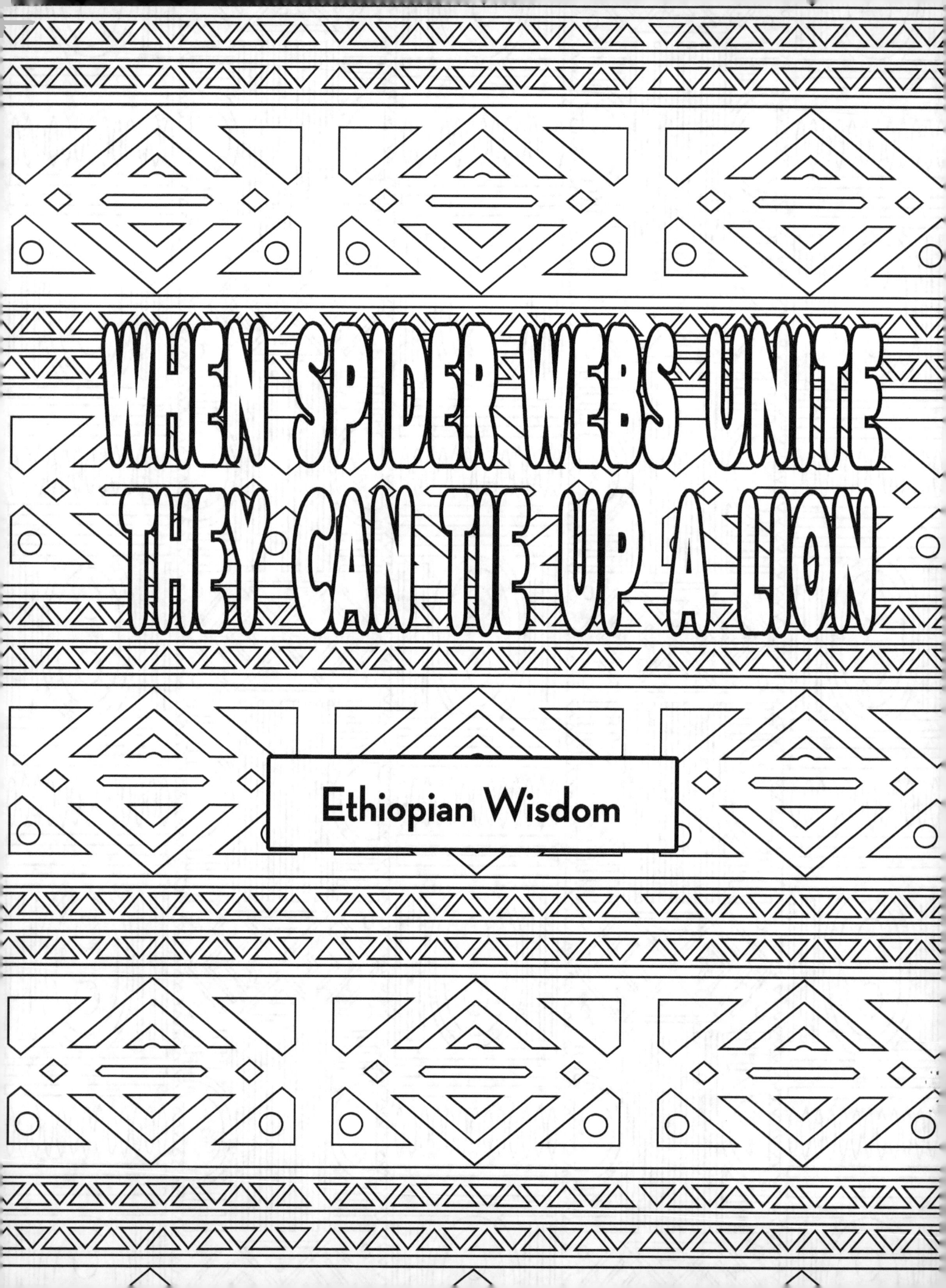

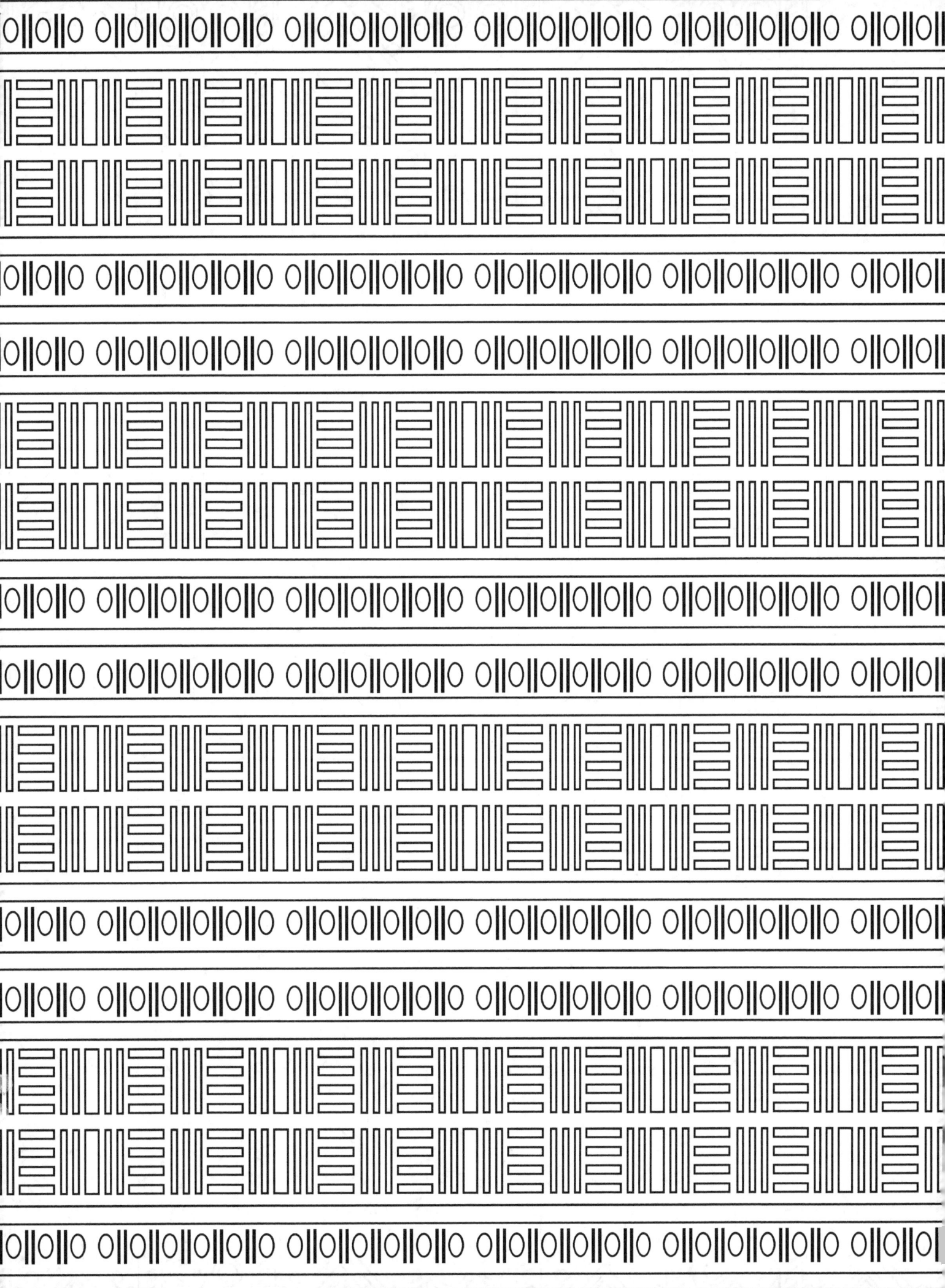

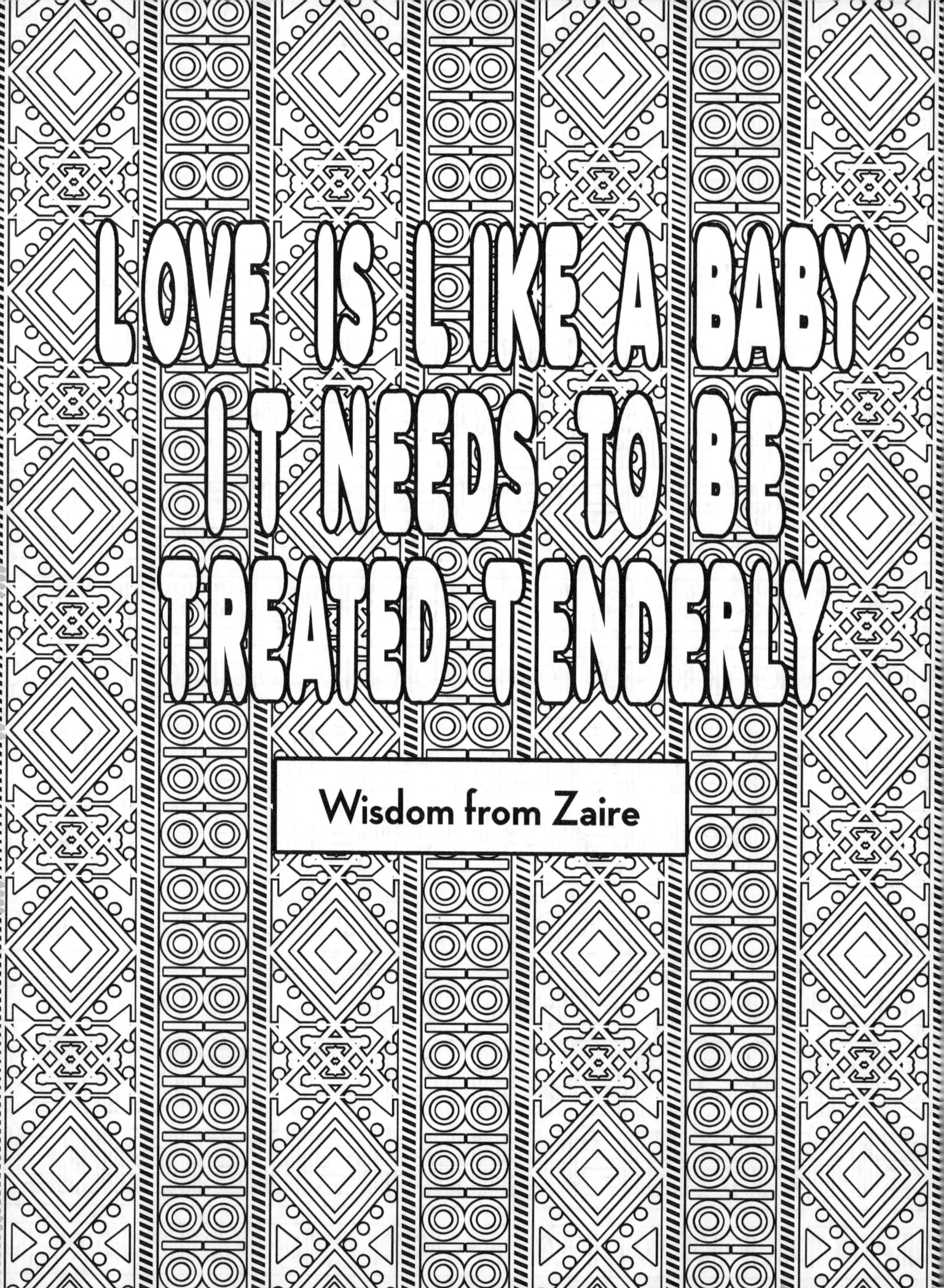

LOVE IS LIKE A BABY
IT NEEDS TO BE
TREATED TENDERLY

Wisdom from Zaire

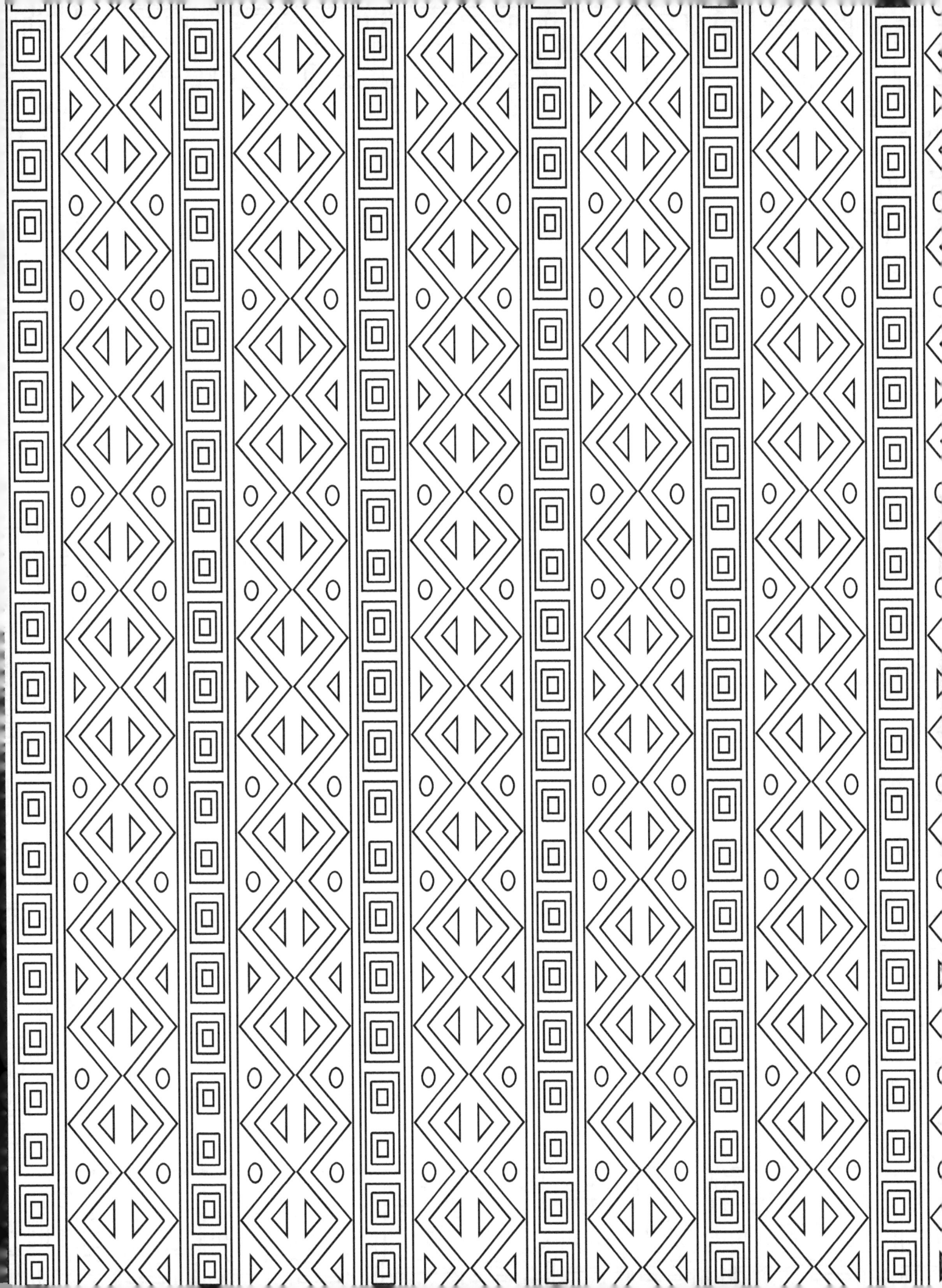

NOTES

NOTES

NOTES

NOTES

LADY KHADIJA is an Early Childhood Educator by trade, an artist by calling, and an advocate by nature.

She spends her days developing young minds and teaching life-skills, entrepreneurship, and business development to grown folks. She spends nights writing, designing graphics and web sites, and performing poetry.

She runs a safe place for women and children, owns and operates two blogs, and manages to slip some time in as a blog and social media consultant.

Find her online at www.LadyKhadija.info

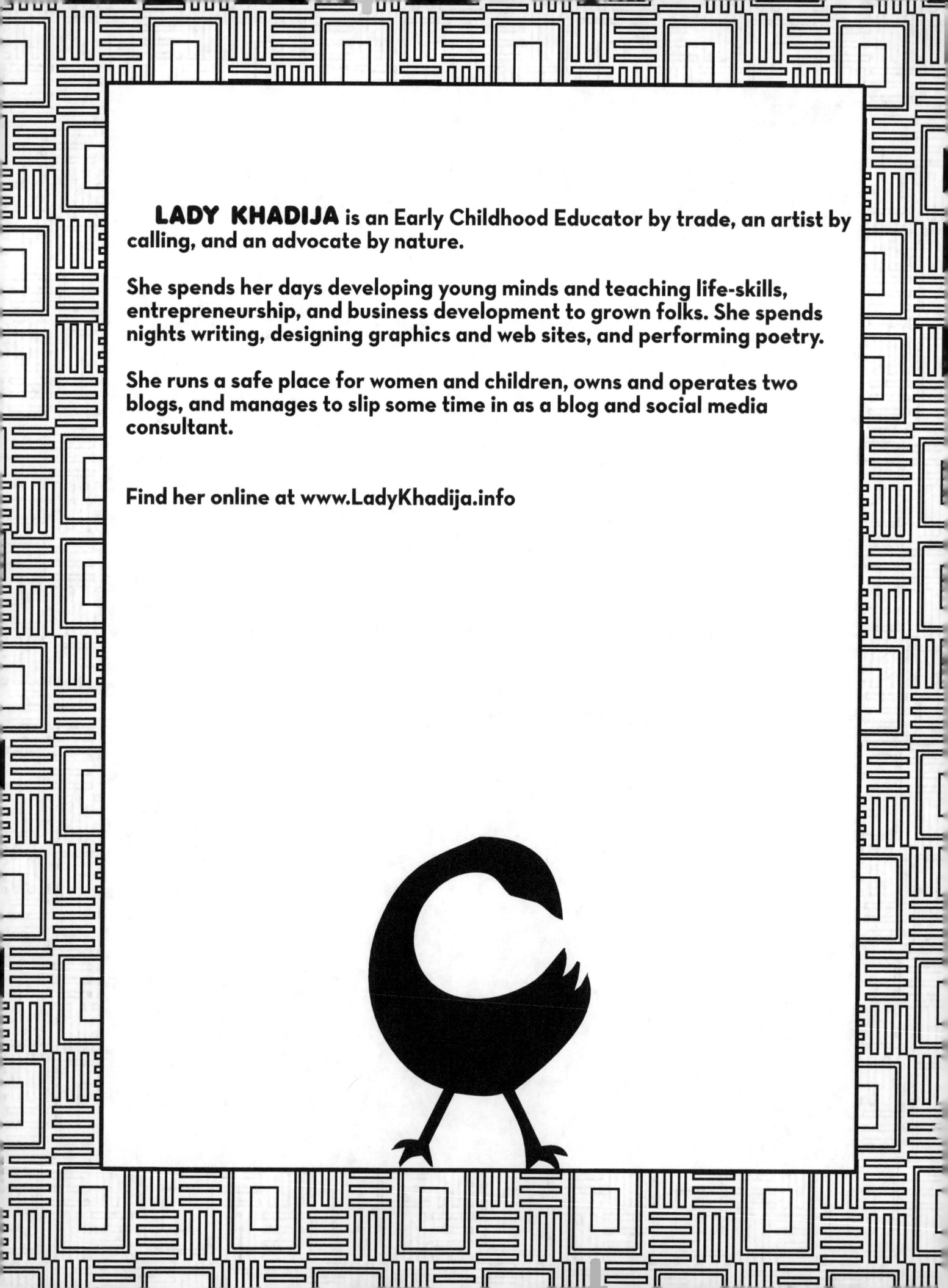

www.ingramcontent.com/pod-product-compliance
Lightning Source LLC
Chambersburg PA
CBHW080606180526
45168CB00007B/2805